CHRISTMAS

AN AMERICAN ANNUAL
OF CHRISTMAS
LITERATURE AND ART

CHRIS

AN AMERICAN ANNUAL OF CHI

EDITED BY RANDOLPH E. HAUGAN · VOLUME FORTY-THREE

KOPIETZ '50

T M A S

STMAS LITERATURE AND ART

UGSBURG PUBLISHING HOUSE · PUBLISHERS · MINNEAPOLIS

TABLE OF CONTENTS

Volume Forty-three

Second Edition

Nineteen Hundred Seventy-three

The Christmas Gospel

Christmas Articles and Stories

Christmas Poetry

Christmas Music

Compiled by Ruth Olson
Artwork by Audrey F. Teeple
Calligraphy by Hildegard Szendrey

Christmas Art

Christmas Illustrators

Joseph Bergeron
Garnet Hazard
Richard I. Heule
Edmund Kopietz
William Medcalf
Lee Mero
Hildegard Szendrey
Audrey F. Teeple
Menzo Van Esveldt

Acknowledgments

Chartres Cathedral: French Government Tourist Office 15
Visitation: E. Houvet 16
Nativity: E. Houvet 17
Shepherds: E. Houvet 17
Adoration of the Magi: E. Houvet 18
North Portal: French Government Tourist Office 19
Royal Portal: French Government Tourist Office 20
South Portal: French Government Tourist Office 21
Ancestors of Christ: E. Houvet 21
Metropolitan Museum, New York, N.Y. 47
Creole Petroleums 48
OAS Photos 48, 49
Museum of New Mexico 50

Manufactured in the United States of America. Library of Congress Catalog Card No. 32-30914

The
Christmas
Story as Recorded
in the Gospels of Saint
Luke and Saint Matthew.

Decorations
by Lee
Mero

AND it came to pass in those days, that there went out a decree from Caesar Augustus that all the world should be taxed. (And this taxing was first made when Cyrenius was governor of Syria.) And all went to be taxed, every one into his own city.

CAESAR

AUGUSTUS

L. M.

NAZARETH

Dothan ⊠

⊠ Geba

Samaria ⊠

Shechem ⊠

⊠ Sychar

Lebonah ⊠

⊠ Bethel

Beeroth ⊠

Gibeon ⊠

Jerusalem ⊠

BETHLEHEM ✡

AND Joseph also went up from Galilee, out of the city of Nazareth, into
Judaea, unto the city of David, which
is called Bethlehem; (because he was of
the house and lineage of David:) to be taxed
with Mary his espoused wife, being great with
child. And so it was, that, while they were
there, the days were accomplished that she
should be delivered.

LM

AND she brought forth her firstborn son, and wrapped him in swaddling clothes, and laid him in a manger; because there was no room for them in the inn. And there were in the same country shepherds abiding in the field, keeping watch over their flock by night. And lo, the angel of the Lord came upon them, and the glory of the Lord shone round about them: and they were sore afraid.

AND the angel said unto them, Fear not: for, behold, I bring you good tidings of great joy, which shall be to all people. For unto you is born this day in the city of David a Saviour, which is Christ the Lord. And this shall be a sign unto you; Ye shall find the babe wrapped in swaddling clothes, lying in a manger. And suddenly there was with the angel a multitude of the heavenly host praising God, and saying, Glory to God in the highest, and on earth peace, good will toward men.

AND it came to pass, as the angels were gone away from them into heaven, the shepherds said one to another, Let us now go even unto Bethlehem, and see this thing which is come to pass, which the Lord hath made known unto us. And they came with haste, and found Mary, and Joseph, and the babe lying in a manger.

AND when they had seen it, they made known abroad the saying which was told them concerning this child. And all they that heard it wondered at those things which were told them by the shepherds. But Mary kept all these things, and pondered them in her heart.

And the shepherds returned, glorifying and praising God for all the things that they had heard and seen, as it was told unto them.

This is according to the Gospel of Saint Luke.

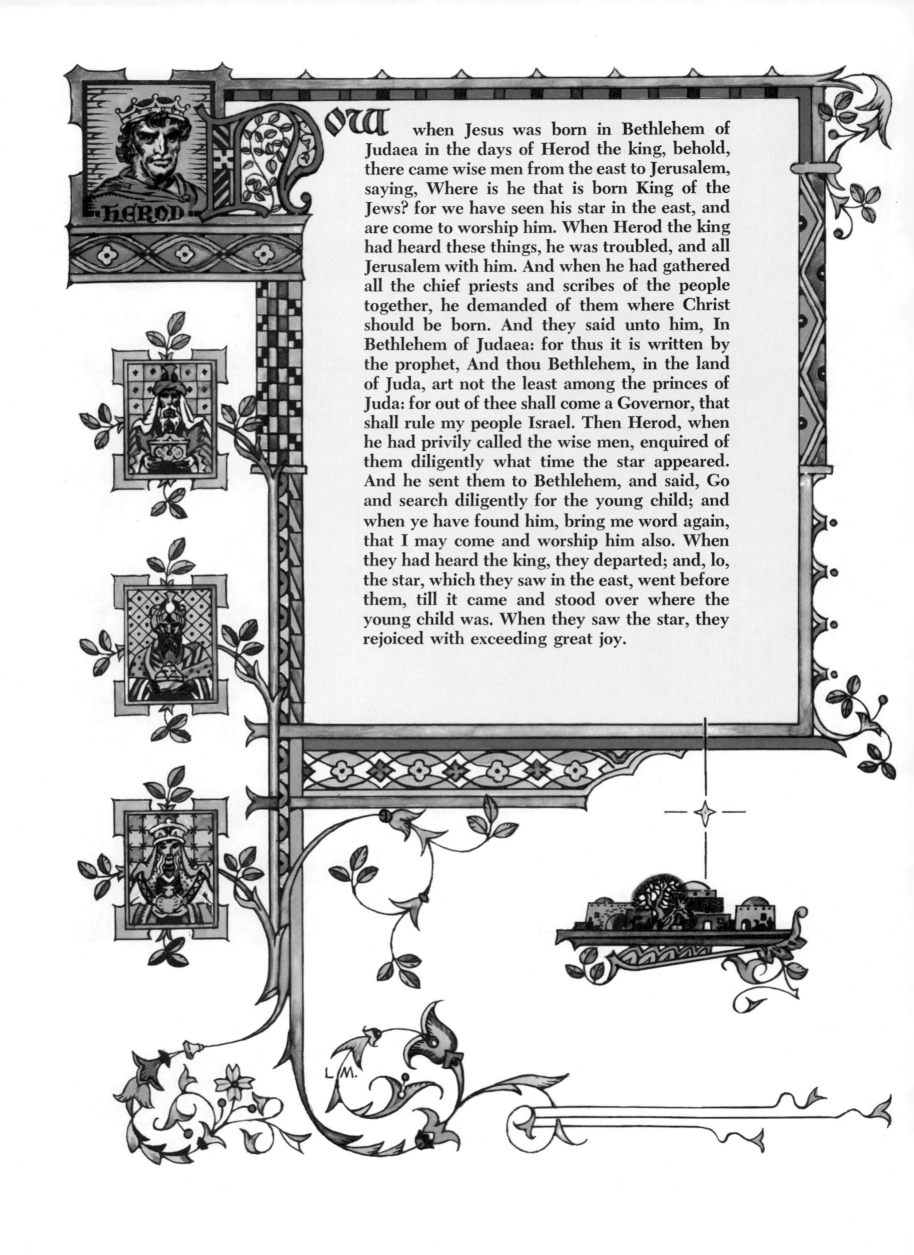

Now when Jesus was born in Bethlehem of Judaea in the days of Herod the king, behold, there came wise men from the east to Jerusalem, saying, Where is he that is born King of the Jews? for we have seen his star in the east, and are come to worship him. When Herod the king had heard these things, he was troubled, and all Jerusalem with him. And when he had gathered all the chief priests and scribes of the people together, he demanded of them where Christ should be born. And they said unto him, In Bethlehem of Judaea: for thus it is written by the prophet, And thou Bethlehem, in the land of Juda, art not the least among the princes of Juda: for out of thee shall come a Governor, that shall rule my people Israel. Then Herod, when he had privily called the wise men, enquired of them diligently what time the star appeared. And he sent them to Bethlehem, and said, Go and search diligently for the young child; and when ye have found him, bring me word again, that I may come and worship him also. When they had heard the king, they departed; and, lo, the star, which they saw in the east, went before them, till it came and stood over where the young child was. When they saw the star, they rejoiced with exceeding great joy.

nd when they were come into the house, they saw the young child with Mary his mother, and fell down, and worshipped him: and when they had opened their treasures, they presented unto him gifts; gold, and frankincense, and myrrh. And being warned of God in a dream that they should not return to Herod, they departed unto their own country another way.

nd when they were departed, behold, the angel of the Lord appeareth to Joseph in a dream, saying, Arise, and take the young child and his mother, and flee into Egypt, and be thou there until I bring thee word: for Herod will seek the young child to destroy him. When he arose, he took the young child and his mother by night, and departed into Egypt: And was there until the death of Herod: that it might be fulfilled which was spoken of the Lord by the prophet, saying, Out of Egypt have I called my son . . .

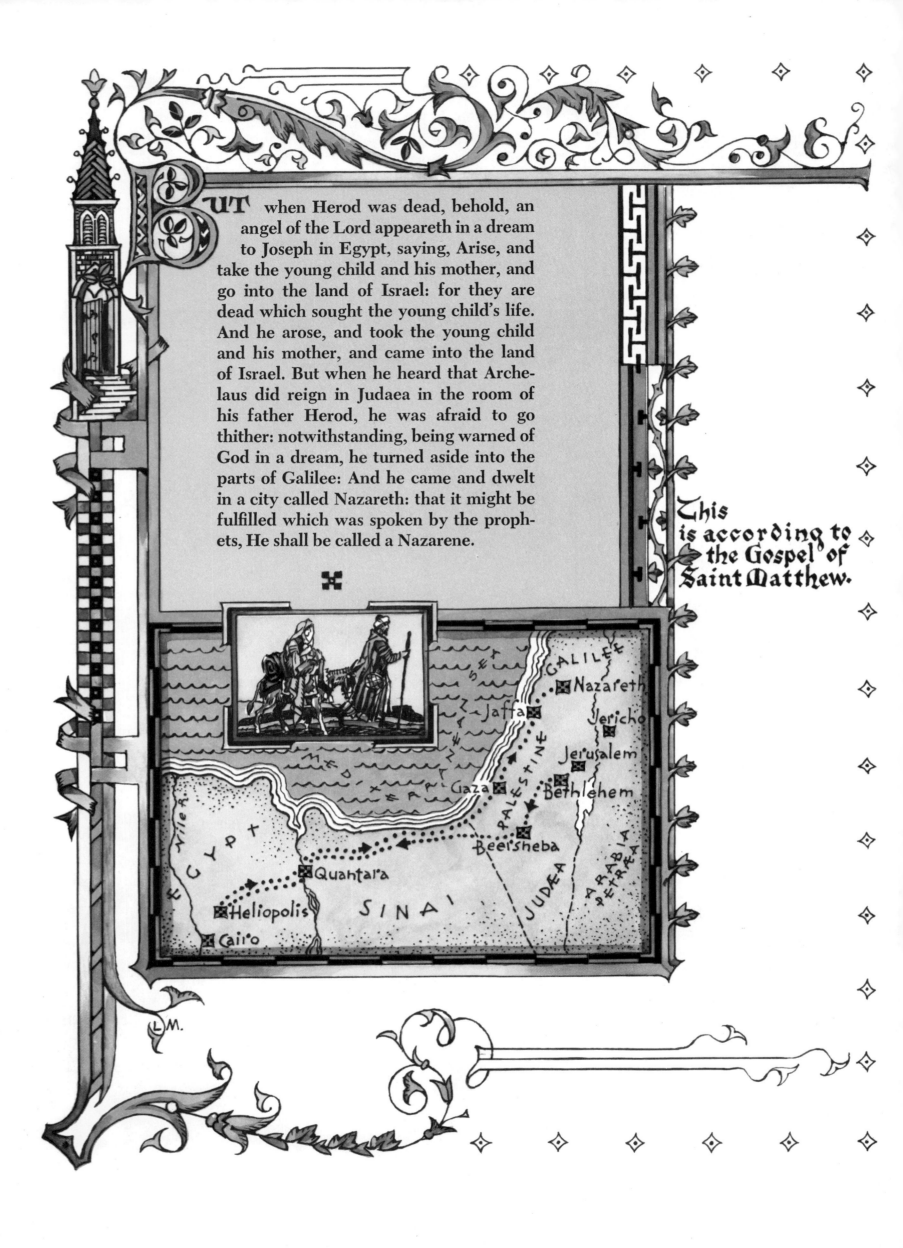

UT when Herod was dead, behold, an angel of the Lord appeareth in a dream to Joseph in Egypt, saying, Arise, and take the young child and his mother, and go into the land of Israel: for they are dead which sought the young child's life. And he arose, and took the young child and his mother, and came into the land of Israel. But when he heard that Archelaus did reign in Judaea in the room of his father Herod, he was afraid to go thither: notwithstanding, being warned of God in a dream, he turned aside into the parts of Galilee: And he came and dwelt in a city called Nazareth: that it might be fulfilled which was spoken by the prophets, He shall be called a Nazarene.

This is according to the Gospel of Saint Matthew.

MANY PILGRIMS have journeyed to Chartres Cathedral in ancient and modern times. The early ones, who traveled by foot or horseback over the plain of Eure, must have rejoiced when they caught their first sight of the cathedral standing on the high ground in the midst of the village of Chartres. Even from a distance the cathedral is overpowering, dominating the town and countryside.

Today's traveler is no less impressed. As he approaches Chartres, whether by automobile or train, he experiences a thrill that combines awe with wonder, realizing that Chartres is one of the great accomplishments of Western civilization.

Coming closer, the traveler perceives that the great church has just two towers: one is lacy and ornate and the other is chastely simple in line. A guidebook tells that the rather plain steeple to the south was finished in 1160, whereas the north tower and steeple was completed in 1513. The years that span the time between these two dates tell the story of how medieval men conceived the plan for building this cathedral that has been so admired for several centuries.

To understand those years is to have a better appreciation of the stones with which men fashioned (quite literally with their own hands) the cathedral and its sculpture. As modern pilgrims, let us go back in time to see the drama of those centuries unfold.

The view of the cathedral is obscured as one approaches the town of Chartres. The houses and shops crowd closely to the church so that they almost screen it from sight for awhile. This was true even in centuries past, for Chartres was a bustling city engaged in active trade created by a textile industry that was the dominant economy. And so the pilgrim then, as now, had to make his way through narrow busy streets to the more open area where the cathedral stands close to the River Eure. The river serves to separate the town from the church and to keep the houses and shops from encroaching completely.

Once in the cathedral, standing a short distance from the West Front, the size of the building and the magnificence of the architecture make its greatest impact. The overall effect is one of grandeur, carried out with simplicity and grace. The eye sweeps over the West Front and is drawn to the main or Royal Portal where three great doors are recessed by tiered arches and numerous columns, all heavily carved with stone sculptures. Even from across the small park in front of the cathedral, one realizes that there are hundreds of these sculptures.

The eye travels upward to a second level, where graceful arches repeat the curve of the portals. Above this is the lacy stone circular enclosure of the great west rose window; and on

The Wonder that is Chartres

JEAN LOUISE SMITH

The Visitation

The church destroyed by the Danes was quickly rebuilt, only to suffer a fire in 1020, 162 years after it had been plundered. This second cathedral experienced other minor fires because of the wooden roof. After each conflagration the people patiently rebuilt.

But now try to imagine, if you will, what the great fire of June 10, 1194 must have been like. The entire town was in danger of being destroyed. The people tried to keep the fire from crossing the Eure River, but the great sparks shot into the air and, carried by the wind, lit on the roof of the church and burrowed into the wood, igniting it. And so the great church fell, the heavy roof pulling down all but the two towers and the West Front. Part of the old crypt where the relic of the virgin was kept was found intact also.

Rebuilding

Imagine how the people felt as they viewed their cathedral in smouldering ashes and rubble! Their thoughts probably moved only slowly from dazed despair to a spark of hope as they began to think about rebuilding. In the memory of all France, Chartres had been a great cathdral — too important to give up now! Enthusiasm for rebuilding was immediate and the people resolved that they would build so well that it would withstand the ravages of centuries to come. The name of Chartres Cathedral would remain forever in the minds of men.

The people were soon speaking of how the church must be even finer than the old one. Those in the town who had traveled far had seen other cathedrals. They had seen St. Denis and Amiens done in the new Gothic style. This meant that instead of needing thick stone walls to give support to the roof and arches, flying buttresses and arches could be constructed outside the walls to help bear the weight. The flying buttresses would not only add grace to the exterior design, but would also enable the builders to make large windows and hence use more stained glass. Light would then pour into the church, flooding the nave with dancing colors of red, green, and blue as the sun shone through the stained glass. The Gothic style was also distinguished by pointed arches and slender pillars, rather than the heavy rounded arches and ponderous pillars of Romanesque style. All of these new features must have been talked about in street and marketplace as the people set about to clear away the rubble.

Before they could begin building, money had to be found. The effort of raising it was to be proven greater than for any previous project they had known. Almost immediately money began to pour in from parishes all over France. It came from former pilgrims and from those who hoped to come to visit the shrine. Vast sums could be counted on from the four fairs, held each year at Chartres in the shadow of the cathedral walls. The church was involved in these fairs for thousands of travelers spent a lot of money on textiles and souvenirs. This meant that all of the local merchants benefited, and they, in turn, gave gifts to the

either side of this, and above, rise the towers with their spires that are like biddings of prayer.

There it is: the exquisitely simple west view of Chartres Cathedral that has stood for about 800 years.

The Fire

The date of 1194 must be well marked, for it was then that the church we see today — except for the West Front — rose from the ashes of the fire that had destroyed the earlier, ninth century church. Even the more ancient church had a predecessor, about which very little is known except that it, too, was a pilgrim church. When, in 858, Danish rovers plundered and destroyed the town of Chartres, there was a church where people came to pray for healing of their bodies at the shrine of a relic, said to be the tunic Mary wore when Jesus was born. They slept in the church, and those who were ill were cared for by the townspeople. The sick were allowed to stay for nine days, and if by that time no healing was manifest, they had to relinquish their places to others. In ancient times the relic at Chartres attracted a constant stream of pilgrims, for the medieval mind was saturated with a love of mystery that is incomprehensible to modern man.

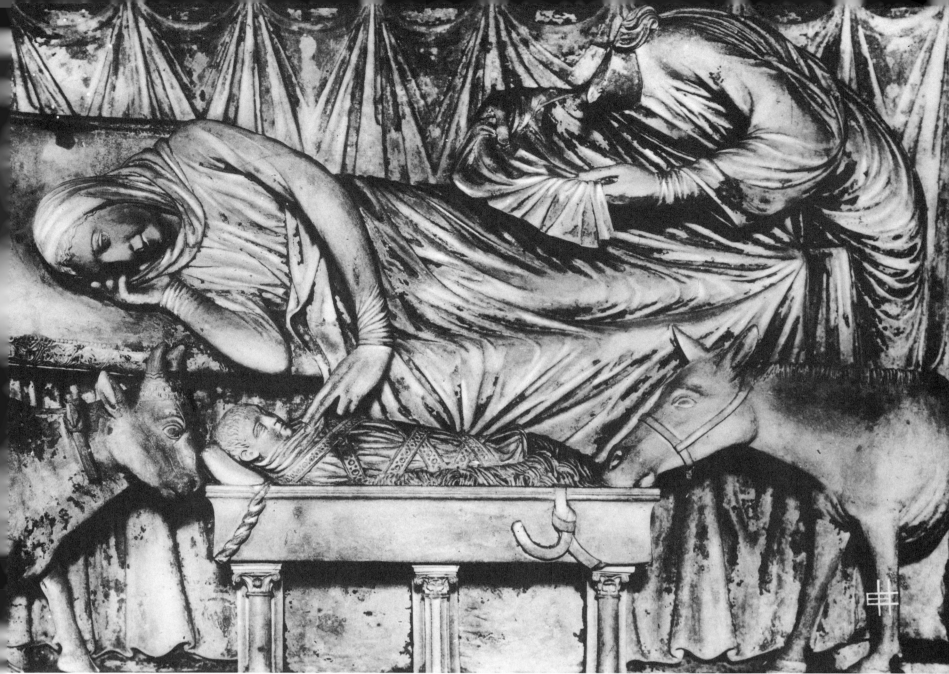

The Nativity

cathedral. Many of the stained glass windows picture and name various guilds who were donors: the butchers, bakers, artisans. Money from this source came in steadily during the 25 years of building. These sources could not be counted on to be sufficient, however, and money was borrowed from the Venetians, the great bankers of all Europe.

Much of the inspiration and help in organizing finances for rebuilding came from Cardinal Melior of Pisa, Italy. The cardinal came to Chartres immediately after he heard of the fire and called the townspeople together. In an inspiring sermon he urged them to forget their sorrow and loss and move ahead with rebuilding. Their famed relic had survived the fire; the people were determined to help; the stone quarries were only five miles distant — so let them build the greatest cathedral in France, perhaps in all the world, he said. The work was to begin within a year after the fire, as soon as a master builder was found.

If the name of the master builder were known he would be talked about as one of the world's greatest architects! But strangely enough, his name is not known — no hint of it survives in the account books, nor is it inscribed on any of the stones of the cathedral. Much information is available about how he worked, but not his name. The bishop of the chapter was, of course, the over-all supervisor, but the master builder,

There were Shepherds abiding in the fields

The ravages of time show clearly in this grouping of the Magi

working under him, organized and supervised a huge working staff of several hundred people. Within 25 years this man designed the cathedral, directed the raising of walls and roof, assembled and trained the artists and craftsmen who did the stone carvings and the stained glass windows. Hopefully, he lived to see the task completed.

Light and harmony were the keys to his design. The new church was in plan and proportion like the old one, but with a far lighter appearance both inside and out. An old miniature was found in a nearby monastery where monks, engaged in making handprinted books, had decided to paint a rather large miniature on one page. Perhaps the monk had just come from hearing the bishop preach in Chartres Cathedral. Whatever the scene was that inspired him, he set down a detailed painting of an important clergyman preaching in Chartres. He included considerable detail of the interior of that ninth-century church — enough so the master builder could follow it in 1194 to preserve what he wished of the older building. For the rest, he had to rely on the memories of the people.

Standards of work were high in those days, but for building a cathedral like Chartres, the quality of work was set at an unbelievable level. No short-cuts were allowed either in labor or material. Each person engaged in doing the handwork was expected to do his best, and his devotion in doing it was to be beyond reproach. Volunteers came forward by the hundreds, not just from Chartres, but from all France, since it was considered an honor to have a hand in rebuilding such an important cathedral. It is said that even the wealthy and nobles allowed themselves to be harnessed to carts that drew stones from the quarry outside the town. They also learned to shape the stones and set them in place; some developed a talent for doing the sculpture and working with stained glass.

So responsive were people in all levels of society to the call to rebuild, that the work moved ahead speedily, considering the scope of the task. The roof was put on in 1220, and, though there was much to be done after that, everything except some of the minor work was accomplished by 1260. The result was what Henry Adams called the most perfect piece of architecture in the world.

How one wishes that a record had survived of the festivals and services of worship held in the cathedral after its completion! Noblemen, clergy, and lay-people came from all over France to take part. The imagination needs but a slight spark to kindle a vision of what the festivities might have been like, with great processions, banners, and song.

The cathedral was literally regarded as the house of God, and churches were believed to be symbolic of the kingdom of God on earth. Thus, to build a church —particularly a cathedral like Chartres—was to translate this belief into stone so that every part of it would witness to the Christian faith.

Rather than end our story with the dedication of the new Chartres Cathedral, the modern pilgrim is invited to look more closely at the witnessing stones. He can enjoy and understand them better against this background of their history. A busload of tourists, making a two-hour stop at Chartres, is dazzled by the sight of such beauty. The imagination is simply staggered by the sight of it all. What they want next, is some help in identifying and appreciating what they see as they stand before each of the three great portals of Chartres.

The Royal Portal—West Front

The West Front with its Royal Portal is often called "The Gate to Heaven." In his series *Civilisation*, Lord Kenneth Clark says that Chartres Cathedral is the epitome of the first great awakening of European civilization. He speaks of the sculptured portals as being the most impressive in the Western World. It takes no stretch of imagination to agree with this. These sculptures, it will be remembered, are earlier than those of the North and South Portals, for they predate the fire of 1194. This places them in the second third of the twelfth century. Compared to the carved figures of the other two portals, those of the West Front may seem stiff and rigid in posture. But look at their faces. They have what one historian calls "quality of soul," and this is seldom found in sculpture, for stone does not lend itself to the nuances and fine shadings which painting permits.

More than 700 figures of people and animals are carved on the West Front! Most prominent are the tall statues that stand so regally against the columns on either side of the three entrances. Nineteen of them remain out of the original 24. They stand like motionless kings and queens, witnessing to their faith. Their arms are close to their sides or clasped in attitudes of prayer. They represent important Old Testament personages, all of whom cannot be identified for certain. But among them are Ruth, Boaz, Solomon, Jesse, and David. They are there to begin the drama of the coming of Christ to the world — the theme of the West Portal.

The North Portal

Royal Portal

A noble figure of Christ is carved over these figures. It fills the space under the great arch above the door and shows him seated on a throne; a man in the prime of life and having an expression that is strong in its depth and seriousness.

Carvings are everywhere on the doorjambs, on the smaller shafts that are part of the structure of the arches, on the lintels, the recessed arches. Some of these are of important events such as the scene showing the Infant Jesus being presented at the Temple when a small baby. He is surrounded by his kinsfolk with their offerings of doves.

Close to this is the scene showing the Presentation in the Temple. Close by is one of the several sculptured nativity scenes that are pictured in stone and in stained glass at Chartres. This particular one is well-loved for the group of shepherds clad in their medieval style tunics and leggings. They stand at the foot of the bed as they pipe joyful tidings on their curious pipes. Their dog and a few sheep are with them.

Lesser subjects of the West Front carvings include the signs of the zodiac, each with its appropriate labor; the seven liberal arts — considered important in medieval theology — are there to declare God's created plan for the world. There are little everyday scenes of harvesting, of musicians with their instruments, and of wild and domestic animals. These served to remind the people that everything that happened in their own lives, everything they knew about, witnessed to the Creator who sent his Son into the world.

The North Porch

The sculptures of the North Porch further tell of the coming of Christ to the world. Each of the statues has a part in carrying out this theme, beginning with the ancestors of Christ and continuing through various events up through his Nativity. The lineage follows faithfully the list in St. Matthew's gospel. A great Tree of Jesse is carved over the central doorway of the North Porch to signify the lineage through David.

Below the Tree of Jesse, over the central door, are large statues of the patriarchs. Melchizedek (see Hebrews 5:6), as both a priest and a king, is a type of Christ. He is shown crowned and holding a chalice in his left hand and a censer in his right. A lamb, symbolizing the Lamb of God, is at his feet. This figure is considered to be an especially fine piece of carving and in an excellent state of preservation.

Abraham stands next to Melchizedek, appropriately holding the knife in his right hand while with his left he strokes Isaac's head. The sacrifice of Isaac by Abraham is considered a type of the sacrifice of the Son of God. Moses stands next to Abraham, holding the tablets of the law and lifting up the rod which has a serpent entwined on it. Next, is Samuel holding a sacrificial lamb, and finally, David, also a type of Christ, carrying the instruments of the Passion.

Also on the central bay of the door are smaller carvings of the story of creation and the fall of man. Pillars, capitals, and pedestals are richly carved with events in the Old Testament as related to David, Samuel, and others who witness in some manner as forerunners of Christ.

A beautiful Visitation is carved along a column of the left doorway of the North Portal. Done with simplicity and great dignity, it shows Mary coming to visit her cousin Elizabeth. The easy grace and natural lines of these two figures makes it difficult to believe that they were done in the thirteenth century. Above, in a sculptured arch, are several scenes to show the birth of Jesus, the shepherds, and the Wise Men.

As on the West Front there are about 700 figures carved on the North Porch. All of them together tell the story of the coming of Christ. The statues are natural in proportion and more life-like than those of the West Front, and hence they appeal to us today somewhat more readily than the older ones. It is appropriate that these engaging personages, so warm and human, should have been chosen for the cold northern exposure where the sun never shines.

The South Porch

The South Porch is given over to carvings of the Christian martyrs and to the Last Judgment. In fact, the porch is sometimes referred to as the Martyr's Portal. The Last Judgment is carved above the great central door quite realistically to show the blessed and the condemned. The door to the left shows the martyrs of the church as coming from all levels of society and from the beginnings of the Christian Church. The right entrance is known as the Confessors Portal for

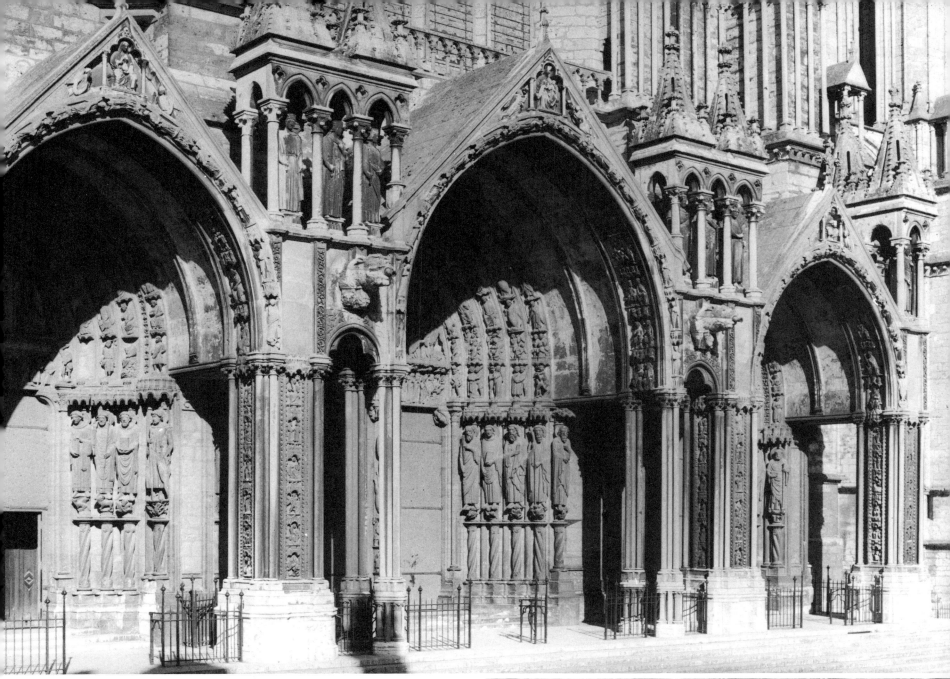

The South Portal

carved on it is the splendid company of those in the early church who defended the faith and testified to it: Ambrose, St. Nicholas, St. Martin, Jerome, and others. Each is shown accomplishing a significant act associated with his life and work.

The South Portal is loved for its beautiful statue of Christ known as the "Beau Dieu." It stands in a prominent position and is easy to view as one mounts the steps to enter the cathedral. For the people of the fifteenth century this Christ, as one who tramples evil, was something of a new conception. The wonderfully human yet spiritual face of this Christ so warmed the hearts of the people that they looked upon it and felt closer to him than they perhaps felt on looking at the formal, kingly Christ enthroned over the West Portal.

And so the very stones of Chartres Cathedral have witnessed the coming of Christ to the world for many centuries. They witness also to the faith and love of the people — those artisans, sculptors, and builders who gave their best to create what many consider to be the most beautiful cathedral in the world!

Ancestors of Christ—
Melchizedech, Abraham, Moses,
Samuel and David

Poems of Christmas

Old Shepherd, Remembering

"You are too old for tending flocks of sheep,
Especially at night," they tell me now,
The younger shepherds. "You would fall asleep
Or stumble in the dark." If they could know
The hunger in my heart to be again
Within that field beneath the starlit sky!
It's lonely when you are the only one
Still living who beheld the angels high
And radiantly fair, who heard their voices.
But oh, I know with flaming certainty
That I shall hear them, see those angel faces
Again. How bright, how glorious they will be
In vaster skies, in realms of loveliness
Beyond what earthbound hearts can dream or guess!

GRACE V. WATKINS

Joseph's Prayer

God, please protect this Holy Child,
   and help me play the part
I am assigned. Oh, make me mild
   of tongue and strong of heart!

Let me not scorn the man who said
   "No room," and shut his door . . .
You led us to this cattle shed
   where gentle Mary bore

the Prince of Peace. A palace room
   might frighten shepherd folk
who shy at grandeur. Stable gloom
   dispersed when Christ awoke!

Quicken my pace if we must flee,
   O Lord; and let me know
which land will hide your Son when he
   is hunted by a foe.

Make me a vessel of your grace.
   Let naught be sheltered there
but thoughts that I would gladly trace —
   desires the Child could share.

ARLYLE MANSFIELD LOSSE

Oratorio

In the magnificent distance,
There commenced an overture of love
More delicate than the natural song of birds,
Profoundly beautiful.
The murmur of sound grew strong on the wind,
Heralding the hope of peace to mankind,
Long-deafened by the discord of human living.
A crescendo of glory swept through the skies,
Resonant in the hills and
Majestic in perfect harmony.
The choir revealed a new psalm, complete —
Blessed in the cry of a baby.
Man's ear was attuned, at last,
To an eternal song.

JUDITH MATTISON

Fulfillment

Did Mary wonder that the light
Was bright so she could see
Her new-born son upon her lap
And wrap him properly?

And did she watch him growing tall,—
By all beloved and blest,
And try to comprehend that he
Could be God, manifest?

Perhaps she wove with loving care
And prayer, forebodingly,
The seamless robe that Jesus wore,
Footsore to Calvary.

Did Mary keep the gift of myrrh
With her through all the years,
And carry it to Jesus' tomb —
Perfume, instilled with tears?

Ah! When she saw the Risen Lord
Restored at Easter-tide,
All she had pondered in her heart,
Apart, was glorified:

The star! The cross! The holy light —
So bright that she could see
Divinity upon her lap
And wrap him tenderly!

VERA B. SWEETLAND

As seen from earth, planets describe intricate loop-like paths on the stationary background of stars. The drawing shows the paths of five planets—Mercury, Venus, Mars, Jupiter and Saturn—over a period of 17 years.

The Star of Bethlehem

KARLIS KAUFMANIS

The charming Christmas story as we find it recorded in the second chapter of Matthew is well known to all of us. Wise Men came from the east to Jerusalem saying, "Where is he that is born King of the Jews? For we have seen his star in the east and are come to worship him." When troubled Herod heard of the strangers, he called the Wise Men and inquired from them what time the star appeared. Then he told them, "Go and search for the Child, and when you have found him, come and tell me so that I may come and worship him also." When the Wise Men departed from the king, a miracle took place: the star they had seen in the east was in the sky again, and it went before them till it came and stood over where the Child was.

This brief statement is all we know about the Christmas star. It may come as a surprise to some readers, for it is generally believed that our knowledge about the star and the ancient event itself is much more profound. We can't even be so sure that the Christ Child was visited by *three* Wise Men, as pictures on Christmas cards and countless pieces of poetry try to convince us. The only source of information we have is the Gospel of Matthew, and it does not say a word about the number of the visitors.

But every time Christmas rolls around, people keep wondering about the nature of the star. What was it? A divine phenomenon? A regular astronomical show? Or just a creation of imagination to envelop the Christmas story in a legendary light?

Planets Versus Stars

If the Bethlehem star, indeed, was a divine phenomenon, then an astronomer, of course, has nothing to say. But Babylonian writings and mathematical computations inform us of an extremely rare event that took place in the night sky about the time Jesus was born. The unusual celestial display was so beautiful and awe-inspiring that it was noticed and described even by stargazers who were other than Jewish. From the striking resemblance between what happened in the sky and the message of Matthew, it is reasonable to believe that the story of the star was coincidental with the ancient celestial show. To understand it, however, a few simple astronomical and astrological ideas must be introduced.

We recall from our school days that stars are distant suns. They spend their long cosmic lives so far in space that tens, hundreds, and even millions of years elapse before their light reaches us. Because of the

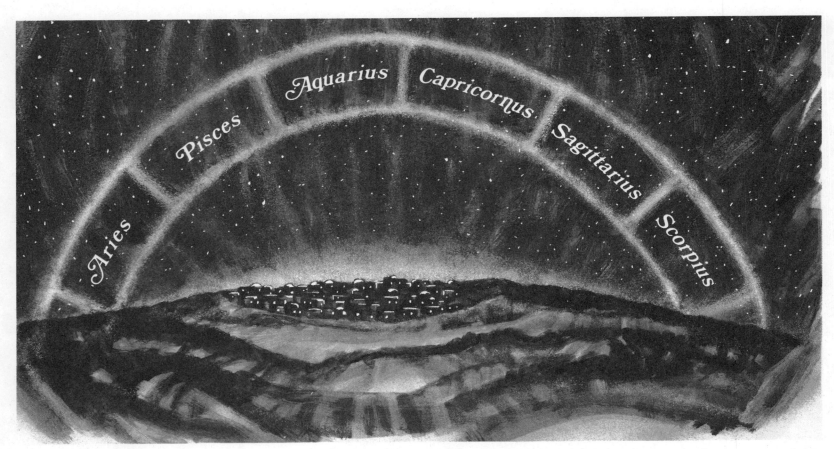

The paths of the sun, Jupiter, Saturn and most of the other planets are confined to a narrow belt in the sky—the zodiac. Six zodiac signs are seen in the drawing, the other six are below the horizon.

tremendous distances involved, stars appear like stationary, motionless points in the sky. This is why The Great Dipper, Orion, and other constellations look tonight exactly as they did a year or 10 years ago, and we have every reason to believe that they will remain that way for many centuries to come.

But, in addition to stars, the night sky is frequently decorated by nearby luminaries called planets. Being members of our own solar system, they revolve faithfully about the sun and thus excel themselves on the stationary background of the starlit sky.

Little Bits of Jewish Astrology

There is nothing mysterious about their loop-like paths. The laws governing the planetary motions are known so well that the positions of planets can be determined centuries in advance. But this was not the case 2000 years ago. As the ancient stargazers watched the sky, their attention was naturally caught by the swiftly moving planets rather than the "stationary" stars. As a result, a group of pseudoscientists called astrologers came into existence who asserted that the positions and motions of luminaries reveal future happenings. Everything is written in the sky, they claimed; one just must know how to interpret the celestial language.

Although astrologers have no scientific basis for their claims, it must be admitted that astrology has at times exerted a profound influence on human minds. It seems possible that the story of the star of Bethlehem coincides with an old Jewish astrological belief. But to understand the argument, three facts must be kept in mind.

First, two planets, Jupiter and Saturn, had a particular importance in Jewish astrology. Jupiter was called the King's star, while Saturn was believed to be the star of the Messiah. Prophet Amos called it "the star of gods," and an old Jewish saying asserted that God had created Saturn to shield Israel.

Second, the sun and most of the planets move in such a way that they never leave the zodiac, a narrow band that stretches across the sky. The ancient stargazers divided it into 12 equal blocks or signs. The sun passes through all of them once a year, Jupiter does the same job in 12 years, while Saturn, moving at a leisurely pace, takes 30 years to complete the trip.

To modern astronomers, zodiac signs are just rectangular areas in the sky used to describe positions of the sun and planets. To Jewish astrologers, however, they symbolized 12 different countries. The most important among them was the Sign of the Fish believed to represent Palestine. No wonder then that many ancient astrological writings refer to it as the House of the Hebrews.

As the swiftly moving sun glides through the zodiac signs, it overtakes Jupiter and Saturn once every 13 months or so. When this happens, the planet disappears in the glare of the sunlight. With the passing of time, however, the distance between the sun and the planet increases, and the day comes when the planet emerges in the eastern sky shortly before sunrise. Known as the heliacal rise, the first appearance of the planet in the rays of the dawning day had a particular importance in Jewish astrology.

Taking all this into consideration, Jewish astrologers predicted that the Messiah's coming will be heralded

by a simultaneous heliacal rise of Jupiter and Saturn at the House of the Hebrews. This astrological belief was highly supported by an old but erroneous legend which asserted that a similar phenomenon had announced the birth of Moses.

When one considers how passionately the oppressed Jews longed for their deliverer, he can well imagine that their astrologers had never before waited for the heliacal rise of Jupiter and Saturn in the House of the Hebrews with such an impatience as they did about the time when Jesus was born. And then— after more than 853 years—there came the long awaited conjunction again! For more than eight months both planets remained side by side and during this time they passed each other three times.

The Magnificent Celestial Show

The magnificent celestial display took place in 7 B.C. During the first part of that year, Jupiter and Saturn were hiding themselves in the glare of sunlight and nothing seemed to indicate the approach of the grand event. But then it came. On the morning of April 12, shortly before sunrise, both planets emerged in the rays of the glowing dawn and—what was equally important—they were in the House of the Hebrews! Already close to each other, they kept getting nearer

and nearer. When on May 27 faster moving Jupiter passed Saturn, the distance between them started increasing and it appeared that the show had come to an end. But astrologers did not realize that another surprise was in store for them. In the middle of July, both planets stopped the motion of recession and once more closed the distance between them during late September and early October, shedding upon earth their double brilliance throughout the nights. The 5th of October was the peak of this very rare celestial show. Separated by a distance of less than two diameters of the moon, the two planets formed an unforgettable scene in the dark October skies of the Middle East. The distance between them increased then a little until mid-November, when the planets started moving toward each other for the third time to reach the closest position on December 1. From then on, a new and this time a final withdrawal took place. Before they disappeared in the rays of the sun, however, they were joined by Mars, thus giving this unusually long and impressive parade of planets a grand and spectacular conclusion. But Mars, according to Jewish astrology, was the greatest enemy of their nation. One can well imagine how disappointed Jewish astrologers must have been when toward the end of the bright and prom-

ising display of the two friendly planets the symbol of ill omen entered the scene.

Was Jesus Born 1973 Years Ago?

This is what happened in the sky in 7 B.C. To see the probable connection between this event and the star of Bethlehem, we have to keep in mind that Jesus was not born 1973 years ago. Our calendar is based on computations of Dionysius, a 6th century monk, who calculated that Christ was born 753 years after the accepted date of the foundation of Rome. He erred.

It is known from Scripture that Jesus was born during the reign of Herod. But historians tell us that Herod died at least four years before the beginning of the Christian era. This brings the date of Jesus' birth close to the time when the triple conjunction of Jupiter and Saturn took place.

How the Star Guided the Wise Men to Bethlehem

What we have discussed up to now are hard facts based on mathematical and historical evidence. However, to restore the ancient event as it might have happened in those olden days, a little bit of imagination can be used.

First of all, who were the Wise Men from the east? Three kings? Rich pilgrims searching for the new-born Messiah? There seems to be little doubt that the men were Jewish astrologers from Babylonia who had followed the planetary motions watching for the signs that would confirm the birth of the Messiah foretold by the prophets. But they had to wait for a long time. It was not until April 12, 7 B.C., that the heliacal rise of Jupiter and Saturn took place in the House of the Hebrews. When the planets met for their first conjunction, on May 27, there could not be any further doubt: the long-awaited Messiah had been born in Palestine.

It was now their duty to go to Jerusalem to find the message of joy. Since, however, the month of May marked the beginning of the hottest season in Palestine, it is likely that the astrologers postponed their trip across the desert until the cooler months of

fall. And when they had the second conjunction—on October 5—even more impressive than the first one! —it must have encouraged them to leave immediately for Jerusalem.

Having spent from five to six weeks on their journey, the Wise Men could have reached Jerusalem by the middle of November. Their inquiries for the new-born King of the Jews brought them eventually to Herod, who asked them about the time the star had appeared.

From Herod's conversation with his high priests and the astrologers, we gather that the star could not be seen by this time. That agrees with the astronomical data, for by mid-November the planets were far away from each other. But while the Wise Men tarried in Jerusalem, the planets moved once more together, and on December 1—for the third time this year!—came to a conjunction. After sunset, the stars of the Messiah and the King would be seen side by side south of Jerusalem in the direction of Bethlehem, which was only a few miles away.

If the astrologers really followed the star, in about two hours they could have reached a place where the road turned southwest. But by this time, both planets had also turned westward and gleamed magnificently over the roofs of Bethlehem. Thus, the astronomical calculations agree amazingly with the message of the Gospel, " . . . and, lo, the star, which they saw in the east, went before them, till it came and stood over where the young Child was."

+   +   +

This is the story of the star of Bethlehem as seen by an astronomer. Milleniums separate us from the days when the Wise Men carried the message of joy across the desert of Mesopotamia. But the yearnings of man for a richer and more perfect life have not ceased since then. He still longs for peace, freedom, friendship and love. Despite the waves of evil and hostility that cross our planet now and then, the message of Christmas has lost none of its significance during the march of centuries, and the Christmas star shines above us with the same unceasing light as it did nearly 2000 years ago.

CHRISTMAS
IN THE COUNTRY
"Once upon a time"

A few days before Christmas, the team was hitched to the bob-sled and the folks drove in to the village,

Illustrations by LEE MERO

They did their trading at the General Store

while Grandfather talked with "old cronies" 'round the stove.

A mail-order box was picked up at the depot; — And then, — back home, mysterious packages were locked in the bedroom closet; —

With Christmas a few days away, the baking began, And sweeping and dusting;

The Parlor was opened for the first time since Thanksgiving!

Fresh husks were put in the bed-tick for the spare room

The lamps were filled and their chimneys were shined—

An extra lot of wood was sawed and split,

and Grandfather kept an appointment with the fattest goose, out behind the barn.

Hams and bacon were taken from the smoke-house,

Fresh butter was churned

(not forgetting that goose-grease was "just awful good for boots,— and poultices")

Everybody was a-flutter when the relatives arrived "from the city" the day before Christmas!

After supper, all went to the church for the children's program.

The youngsters gave their recitations

BLESSED CHRISTMAS

and got popcorn balls and candy!

Back home again,— the Tree was lighted and Grandfather read the Christmas Story according to the Gospels of St. Luke and St. Matthew.

And,— then, there were gifts for all!

The parlor stove was filled for the night—

And in the kitchen, the buckwheat batter was stirred up and put at the back of the stove "to set."

Tabby curled up in her favorite corner.

Then the children piled into cold beds up under the rafters,

Early Christmas morning, the sound of the coffee grinder meant, "EVERYBODY UP," because no one wanted to be late for the morning service.

After church, the Pastor and his family came for dinner.

The Oldsters spent the afternoon visiting

and picked the names for next year's gifts.

But Grandfather just snoozed!

while the youngsters took to hill and pond

In the evening, everyone enjoyed the magic-lantern slides, — (shadow pictures were fun, too!)

followed by sandwiches in the kitchen, (good) and "left-overs! (um-m-m)

Time passed all too soon for the folks who had to get back to the city."

The whole family piled in to the bob-sled for the ride to the depot, — "Number Four at 11.47 was always on time!"

(a requested reprint)

The Advent of Our Lord

LILY M. GYLDENVAND

EACH year the children of God of all ages look forward with eager expectant joy to the coming of our Lord Jesus Christ. Throughout the four weeks of the Advent season, while our hearts and homes are being prepared to welcome him, the excitement mounts.

Among the customs which Christians have established to celebrate this season of hope is the use of the Advent wreath, a lovely symbol that helps us focus attention and devotion upon the One who came in human form at Christmas, who comes by the Holy Spirit through the Word, and who will come again in glory to reign forever.

In the Advent wreath's evergreen boughs we are reminded of the eternalness of God. In its perfect circle his all-encompassing love is symbolized. Each week, as we add the glow of one more candle, we meditate upon another facet of the life and role of our Lord. Candles, which are living flames, are symbolic of Christ, the Light of the World, whose coming is nearer as the light of the candles is increased.

The "Prophecy Candle" is the first candle lit on the first Sunday in Advent. It is symbolic of the long years of waiting during which the prophets, inspired by God, kept alive the hope that the Son of God was coming to redeem the people from their sins.

The "Bethlehem Candle," symbolic of preparation, is added on the second Sunday in Advent. The prophecy in Micah 5:2 that Jesus would be born in Bethlehem, may seem to have been a minor revelation, but it has significance because it indicates how God has prepared even the least detail of the coming of Christ, and ". . . he who promised is faithful" (Heb. 10:23).

The "Shepherds' Candle" reminds us on the third Sunday in Advent of our responsibility to share what we have seen and heard. The Galilean shepherds, who received the first announcement of the Savior's birth, left their task and went with haste to see the Christ child, and then returned to tell others about the earth-shaking event. Sharing the Good News required no special talent—simply telling others what they had seen and heard with the conviction of personal experience. This third candle also serves to recall that Jesus spoke of himself as "the Good Shepherd" who cares for his sheep.

The "Angels' Candle" is lit the last Sunday in Advent. Angels spoke to Mary, to Joseph, and to the shepherds. Angels ministered to Jesus in the wilderness testing and in the Garden of Gethsemane agony. An angel rolled the stone from the tomb and was present with him at his resurrection. Angels are still working in the presence of God and in our midst, protecting, uplifting, guiding God's people along the way.

The Advent wreath is rich in symbolism and, as such, it aids our worship as it reinforces our hope in the ultimate return of our Lord Jesus Christ.

Lullaby for the Child

Night is over the park on
Christmas Eve and an immeasurable
sky full of stars.
I follow winding paths,
my footsteps lighted by the drowsy
lights along the way that have
drawn about them
fragile shawls of fog.

The ground is carpeted with snow,
and walking close
along the darkened shore
I hear the silver melody
of the waterfall,
    falling,
        falling. . . .
chord on chord in sweet remembrance.
It is a lullaby for the Christ Child,
hushed as the wind in fir-trees
this December night.
Its motif is as light as foam of icy lace.
Its gaiety and laughter fall as spray.
And permeating all,
the undertone's unchanging note re-echoing:
"He comes tonight! He comes! He comes!"

Now, back on the bridge,
I see the city's million lights grow
dim, and the tangle of traffic is ended
and quiet settles down.
Kneeling in joy I give thanks
for the night
and its gift:
a lullaby for the Child,
and the assurance that he comes
again tonight.
He comes indeed!

MELVA ROREM

England

CHRISTMAS IN MANY LANDS

Karen F. Olson

England

Many Christian customs popular in England today originated in the Middle Ages when great feasts and celebrations were ordered by kings and noblemen. At these lavish medieval Christmas banquets, the boar's head was ceremoniously brought in and, as a crowning touch, a flaming plum pudding graced the table.

According to tradition, a king and his hunting party became lost in the forest on Christmas Eve. Since they had planned to be at their respective homes in time for the evening celebrations, they had taken only meager provisions with them. They decided to combine these provisions—small amounts of meat, ale, flour, brandy, sugar, and fruit—to make a dish to be shared by all members of the party.

Thus the first plum pudding was made and a proud English Christmas tradition was begun! To continue this tradition, or to add it to your own Christmas celebration, here is my grandmother's plum pudding recipe.

Grandmother's Plum Pudding

1 cup raisins
1 cup currants
1 cup buttermilk
1 tsp. soda dissolved in 1 T. hot water
1/2 tsp. nutmeg
1/2 tsp. cloves
1 tsp. cinnamon
1 tsp. salt
1 cup molasses
3 1/2 cups flour
Mix together in the order given.
Tie the pudding in a clean cloth bag or towel.
Be sure to allow for expansion. Boil in a large kettle of water for 3 hours.

Hard sauce—to be served on the pudding

2 1/2 cups boiling water
Mix together and add all at once to the boiling water:
    1 cup sugar
    2 cups flour
Boil for 5 minutes, stirring occasionally.
Add:
    1/2 cup butter
    1 tsp. vanilla
    2 T. vinegar

Norway

When Norwegian families gather in churches during the Christmas season, one can be sure that music is one of the best loved portions of the worship service. In their vast, ornate cathedrals as well as in their primitive but fascinating stave churches, the Norwegians have told the Christmas story in their beautiful, many-stanzaed hymns.

One of the most cherished of these hymns, one that is passed from generation to generation, is *Jeg er saa glad hver julekveld* (I am so glad each Christmas Eve) which not only tells the story of Jesus but also its meaning for every life.

Also dear to the heart of every Norwegian is *Her kommer dine arme smaa* (Thy little ones, dear Lord, are we). First published in Bishop Pontoppidan's hymnal over 200 years ago, this hymn has brought beauty and blessing to Christmas services the world over.

These two delightful carols are equally well loved in English. But to add a special touch to your Christmas celebration, learn the first verses of these carols in Norwegian, sing them at home around the Christmas tree, and let them bring joy and gladness to your festivities now and in the years to come.

Jeg er saa glad hver julekveld,
ti da blev Jesus født,
da lyste stjernen som en sol,
og engler sang saa sødt.

I am so glad each Christmas Eve,
The night of Jesus' birth!
Then like the Sun the Star shone forth,
And angels sang on earth.

Her kommer dine arme smaa,
O Jesus, i din stald at gaa,
Oplys enhver i sjel og sind
at finde veien til dig ind!

Thy little ones, dear Lord, are we,
And come thy lowly bed to see;
Enlighten every soul and mind,
That we the way to thee may find.

Denmark

Since ancient times, evergreens have been symbolic of eternal life. In Demark, the evergreen is adorned with lighted candles—"living light"—symbolizing the Christmas spirit which continues to fill the hearts of the faithful with peace and joy.

On Christmas Eve, when the festive dinner is over, the parents leave the room to decorate the tree with candles, Danish flags, straw figures, heartshaped ornaments, and stars. Then the doors are opened revealing the gleaming Christmas tree in all its splendor.

The youngest child enters the room first, and soon the whole family gathers in a circle around the tree to sing carols to the one who is the Light of the world. One hymn that is sung in thousands of Danish homes —and indeed throughout the world—is *The happy Christmas comes once more*. This hymn, written by N. F. S. Grundtvig, one of the most prolific hymn writers in the history of Christendom, contains a stanza that picks up the theme of light:

O holy Child, thy manger gleams
Till earth and heaven glow with its beams,
Till midnight noon's broad light hath won,
And Jacob's star outshines the sun.

Norway

Denmark

Switzerland

The snow-clad Alpine mountains and valleys make Christmas a cozy, family-centered festival in this central European republic. For the children there is the visit from the angel-like *Christkindli* who brings gifts of fruit and nuts. Before the children are allowed to play with their toys, the family gathers around the tree to sing the familiar carols, and the story of Bethlehem is read from the family Bible.

Among the inhabitants of the mountain regions, the week between Christmas and New Year's Day is set aside for visiting family and friends. It is a common sight to see two or even three generations gathered in a single house to exchange gifts and share in food and friendship.

Germany

Christmas is observed in Germany with an emphasis on home celebrations and attendance at church services. The observance centers around the Christmas tree, and carols include *O Tannenbaum* and, of course, *Stille Nacht*.

Elaborate preparations are begun weeks in advance —cooking the special meats, and baking bread, fancy cakes, cookies and other special foods.

A Christmas custom that has been preserved in Germany and other European agricultural nations involves giving thanks to God for a fruitful harvest— much like the Thanksgiving Services in the United States and Canada. The Germans make a special bread for this occasion, a bread made of wheat flour, butter, sugar, almonds, and raisins. It is called *Christstollen*. Here is how it is made:

> Stir until dissolved:
> 2 pkg. dry yeast
> 1¼ cup lukewarm water
> Add:
> 1 cup sifted flour
> Permit this to rise in a warm place until doubled.
> Combine in a small paper bag and shake until coated:
> 1 cup raisins
> 8 oz. slivered toasted almonds
> 3 T. flour
> Beat until fluffy:
> 1½ cups butter
> Add gradually:
> 1 cup sugar
> ¾ tsp. salt
> Beat in, one at a time:
> 3 large eggs
> Combine all these ingredients in a large bowl with:
> 5 cups sifted flour

Turn onto lightly floured board and knead until elastic and smooth. Permit it to rise until double in bulk. Punch down. Divide into two or three portions and shape into round loaves. Brush with melted butter and allow to rise, covered, until almost double in bulk. Bake at 350 degrees until well browned—about 45 minutes. Cool on a wire rack and while still warm, brush with lemon glaze.

Lemon Glaze
> Mix together:
> 1¼ cups sifted powdered sugar
> ¼ cup lemon juice
> 1 tsp. grated yellow lemon rind

Holland

In Holland, St. Nicholas Day, December 6, has always been a great day for the children. Nicholas, who was a bishop in the fourth century, now assumes the role of a messenger, coming at the beginning of the Advent season to help the children prepare their hearts so that they can properly welcome the Christ Child at Christmas.

Excitement is high when the ship bearing St. Nicholas arrives. Children hurry on foot or on ice skates, in a frantic race to the harbor. Then, amid shouts of welcome and the ringing of church bells, St. Nicholas disembarks. He asks the children about their behavior, and promises them toys if they have been good.

Sweden

In the midst of winter darkness, the Christmas season begins in Sweden on December 13, St. Lucia's Day. Lucia, a young Christian girl, was martyred in A.D. 303, a victim of the persecution by the Roman Emperor Diocletian. Although Lucia was from Sicily, the story of her kind, thoughtful life and noble death was brought to Sweden by Christian sailors.

Each family chooses its own Lucia who, on this special day, arises earlier than the others, and wearing a crown of lighted candles serves coffee and Lucia buns to the rest of the family. Christmas has now officially begun in Sweden, and the celebrations continue until January 13. These festive observances counteract the darkness as the Christmas spirit brightens every home.

At noon on Christmas Eve day, everyone gathers in the kitchen for *doppa i grytan* (dip-in-the-pot). This custom stems from a famine many winters ago when the only food available was black bread and broth.

Over the fire hangs a large kettle of broth; on the table are slices of dark rye bread. Each person dips a piece of bread into the pot and eats it as a reminder of the famine and also to insure good luck for the coming year.

Christmas Day has for centuries been a day of rest and religious observance. *Julotta*, the pre-dawn worship service, has long been popular on this day. There are still a few people, especially in rural areas, who travel to the church by horse-drawn sleigh, using torches for illumination. The churches also are lit by hundreds of candles, and in this beautiful and peaceful setting the congregation joins in singing a traditional Christmas chorale, such as *How brightly beams the morning star!*

Switzerland

Germany

Holland

Sweden

... and a Time for Creche-watching

ELIZABETH SEARLE LAMB

December is prime time for creche-watching. The manger scene, in various sizes and complexities, appears in shop windows and inside churches; an early Christmas card may show an engraving of the Nativity by an anonymous 12th century German artist or a stylized Holy Family with ox and ass in black silhouette with white halos on a copper background done by a 20th century Chilean artist. At the Metropolitan Museum in New York City, 18th century Neapolitan figures are displayed at the base of a Christmas tree decorated with baroque angels, cherubs, stars and electric candles. In Zipaquira, Colombia, inside the great Catedral de Sal (Cathedral of Salt), carved out of the heart of a mountain in which mining for salt has gone on for hundreds of years, life-size figures are displayed in front of a thatched hut and, above, an angel gleaming against the cold gray salt-rock wall.

The names given to the scene of the manger, lit by a star and peopled by Mary and Joseph and the baby Jesus, are as varied as the representations. 'Creche' has moved into the English dictionaries from the French language, and is used almost as frequently as 'Nativity Scene' or 'The Manger.' The 'Christmas Crib' is the name used in "The Columbia Encyclopedia" which attributes popularity of the custom of displaying the scene of the birth of Jesus to the Franciscans. St. Francis of Assisi, founder of the Franciscan Order, has been credited with originating the custom. 'Presepio' is the term by which the Metropolitan Museum calls its Neapolitan creche, the same name as that used in Brazil and Portugal. In Spanish-speaking countries three words are used: 'Belen,' 'pesebre,' and 'nacimiento.' The first of these, the Spanish 'Bethlehem,' I must take the word of a dictionary for; both of the others I have seen and heard used frequently. 'Pesebre' is the usual term in Colombia; in Venezuela, Dorothy Kamen-Kaye writing in

Christmas Tree, decorated with a collection of Italian (Neopolitan) Christmas crib figures. The Metropolitan Museum of Art, gift of Mrs. Loretta Hines Howard, 1964

47

Venezuela—Parades Fiesta—A Christmas Creche by Razetti

"Caracas Everyday" says both terms are used, 'pesebre' being more usual in the interior of the country, with 'nacimiento' the favored term in Caracas. In Mexico, Central America, Panama and Spain 'nacimiento' is the word most commonly used.

My delight in the manger scene goes far back into childhood, when it was a special privilege to help unwrap the small cherished figures of the Holy Family, the shepherds, the three kings. Perhaps there was a bit of mending to do . . . I seem to remember a couple of lambs which were always losing legs! The display went onto the mantle above the fireplace in the living room, out of easy reach of small children, there to be enjoyed for the Christmas season. However, the first elaborate one I remember was a true nacimiento, a work of art with a village market scene, a river filled with fish, the tropical countryside, all surrounding the focal point of the Nativity scene itself.

This nacimiento was in the home of a friend living in the Panama Canal Zone. At Christmas time it took up most of the living room. Scout troops, school groups, and many many friends visited this nacimiento. And during the rest of the year the nacimiento was far from forgotten. New figures, new features were thought of, and then made . . . tiny birds' nests of little balls of cotton, covered with bits of chicken feathers; a new tile roof for a village house cunningly constructed of match box covers. . . .

Our own nacimiento, the word comes more quickly to mind than creche because it is put together of bits and pieces from countries where the word nacimiento is used, is small and simple in bare fact. It is only behind the fact, in the stories and memories, that there is a web

Venezuela—Parades

of some complexity. The manger itself from a pre-Christmas market set up on the steps leading into the Cathedral of Guatemala City; the figures of Mary and Joseph from a tiny shop in a back street in Belem, Brazil; the baby Jesus, of a size not quite in proportion to the other figures, a replacement made in Puerto Rico; tiny tiny ceramic figures—a hen and infinitesimal chicks, geese and ducks, a squirrel and two cats—these from a market stall in San Jose, Costa Rica. Harp-playing angels in varying sizes, gifts from friends to the harpist in the family. The three kings, a kneeling camel, sheep—the provenance for these is gone. But the grayish moss that drapes over the manger roof and makes a bit of straw in the stable— this comes from Bogota, where it is a Colombian custom to go out each December to gather the moss from the countryside.

Each year I plan to set up the nacimiento nine days before Christmas, and to place the kings far back, moving them closer day by day until they arrive at Bethlehem on Christmas Day. I've never managed it, but perhaps this year? (To be very traditional, the Baby Jesus should be added to the scene late on Christmas Eve; the Magi not arriving until January 6, Dia de los Reyes or Three Kings Day.)

Ecuador—Art nacimiento figures

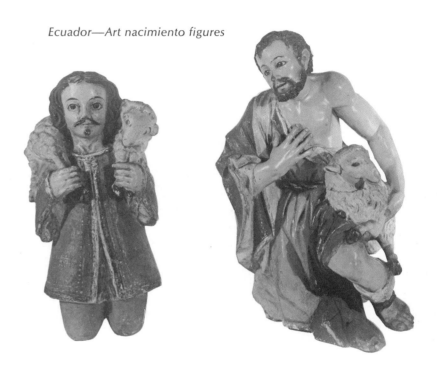

But it is not only at Christmas that one may see the nativity scene. There were the tiniest of little nacimientos, the figures glued in place inside a tiny box, as well as larger carved wooden figures of Mary, Joseph and the infant Jesus, to be found amid the hundreds of folk art or craft objects on sale in the National Center of Arts and Crafts in Mexico City. And my favorite . . . I should say one of my favorites . . . in the exhibit of 400 Santos at the In-

Colombia—Zipaquira Church—Nave of the Nativity

ternational Folk Art Building of the Museum of New Mexico, in Santa Fe, a few years ago, was a beautifully simple Nativity scene. Kneeling figures of Mary and Joseph, both dressed in draped clothing painted in shades of red and black, one on either side of the Christ Child who lay in a small wooden box-crib, date from the 18th century when the art of carving and painting of Santos was flourishing in this area of New Spain. The figures are set in a *nicho*, a kind of shadow box, with painted background dating from a later time.

And the most special one? In Madrid, Spain, making a solitary visit to the house where the Spanish playwright, poet and priest Lope de Vega lived toward the end of his life (1562-1635), the guide brought me finally to the second story room which had been the priest's bedroom. This room had a window opening into the stair well and across into the small *oratorio*, Lope de Vega's private chapel. And there, in a corner, was a charming table-top nacimiento.

When we reached the chapel, the guide and a small black and white cat had made the tour with me, I stood for some time looking at the nacimiento, which was set in a background of dried grayish green pine boughs and holly and other leaves. I asked my guide if he changed the greenery at Christmas time. His answer, as I translated it from Spanish to English for myself, was, "Well, I put some new pieces in once in a while, but I keep it looking old," and he pulled off a couple of pine needles and crumpled them between his fingers to show just how dry and brittle they were. I took one pine needle, myself. It lends, still, the tiniest bit of pine fragrance to my journal. Or do I imagine? At any rate it does remind me that perhaps the secret of any creche is to keep the old, but add just a tiny bit of something new from time to time, so that tradition remains a living thing.

The old and the new—the centuries-old tradition and the now of a living faith—reason, if one be needed, for the habit and the joy of creche-watching.

Nacimiento group made by Fray Anders Garcia, Franciscan who served in New Mexican missions 1748-78

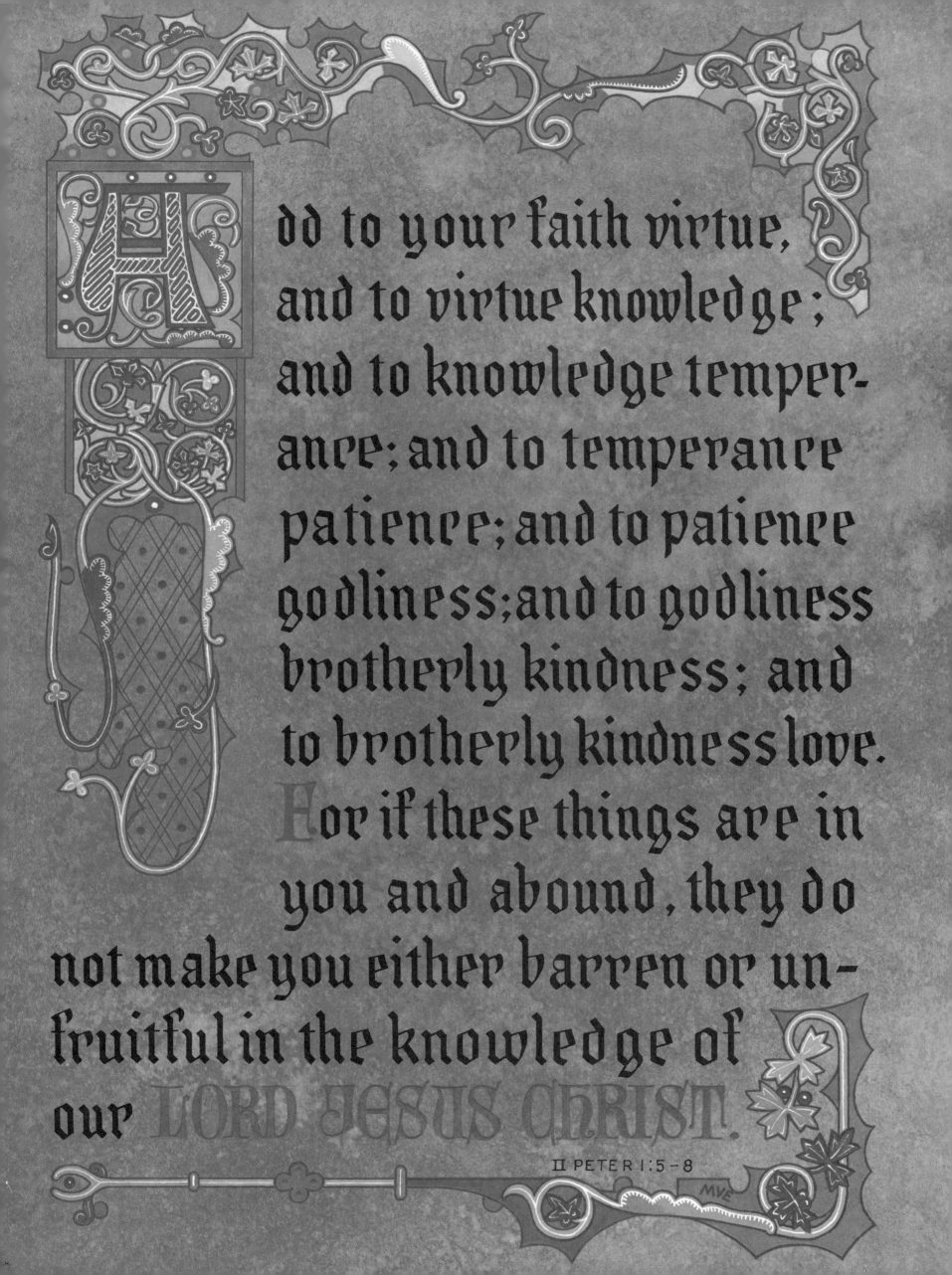

Add to your faith virtue, and to virtue knowledge; and to knowledge temperance; and to temperance patience; and to patience godliness; and to godliness brotherly kindness; and to brotherly kindness love. For if these things are in you and abound, they do not make you either barren or unfruitful in the knowledge of our LORD JESUS CHRIST.

II PETER I: 5-8

A Christmas Letter

ROBERT SHAW

EVERYONE knows what a carol is. At least in this highly stimulated, more than slightly terrifying season of giving and getting (without forgetting) one should certainly be able to recognize a Christmas carol if he heard one.

Well—I'm not so sure. At least I find it very difficult to write a satisfactory definition of a carol. The closer I come to it, the more it appears that most of the churchly tunes with which we in our Sunday school voices ruffled the silent, holy night were not really carols at all—but a species of hymns, in many instances less vital in tune and text than those which I have since come to know as true carols.

In a delightful article in the *Oxford Companion to Music*, Percy Scholes allows that "most of what we call by the name 'carol' would be included in 'a religious seasonal song, joyful in character, in the vernacular and sung by the common people'."

He suggests that there would be an element of *dance*, "for the early carols were danced as well as sung" (perhaps even *before* they were sung, for the word in its medieval French derivation means *round dance*). There would also be an association with the *open air*. (To "go caroling" in my youth meant a Christmas Eve caravan to the cottages of the elderly or ill—obviously those, it occurs to me now, who would benefit more from rest than a shivaree. We would stand outside the bedroom window, on what was usually a clear Southern California night, harmonize tentatively two or three of the familiar Christmas hymns, shout a loud "Merry Christmas," and noisily push off to the next unsuspecting shut-in. We never did accept what they might have wanted to tender, which Mr. Scholes so nicely designates as "hush money.") Carols also would be characterized by *simplicity*, perhaps even *crudity*; and finally by *age*, for the "best carols have served generations of men."

I find myself in sympathy with most of this, except that, in my experience, I find this simplicity more often sensitive than crude. And in instance after instance, both in tune and text, I find a bitter-sweet mingling of the tragic with the joyful: haunting minor melodies, and verses which juxtapose birth and crucifixion.

So it seems to me that there should be a way of stating the *essence* of the carol. How does it differ, for instance, from "Adeste Fidelis" (a magnificent hymn), or "O Little Town of Bethlehem" (by any standards other than auld acquaintance, rather dullish)?

In the first place, the carol is in the direct line of folk music. It *is* "aged," it *is* "in the vernacular and

From **Oxford Companion to Music**, reprinted by permission of Oxford University Press.

sung by the common people"; but this is so precisely because the common people wrote it—a long time ago. Borderline cases exist, but in the main carols were written by no one and by everyone. In the upper corners of the page where credits are inscribed to author and composer, one writes "Traditional . . . Anonymous . . . Unknown."

In the second place (and herein I would guess lies their deep attraction) their origin, anonymous and truly "popular," has wrought a strange amalgam of secular experience and religious story, of Christian and pagan symbolism, of the other-worldly and this-worldly—and all is told in terms naive and profound, simple and surrealistic.

It is not surprising that the Christmas story should inspire this extraordinary mingling. The birth of a child in poverty and oppression, common shepherds granted the first supernatural pronouncement, the royal magnificence of a caravan of kings kneeling in a stable: these are affairs and symbols intuitive to the hearts of men. Here the secular and the sacred do meet and mingle, or, perhaps more truly, speak as though never separate.

A few years ago we recorded a second album of Christmas carols (the first had included the traditional hymns) and the selection of materials was an illuminating experience.

In England, surrounded by seas, one sings unperturbedly of "three ships, sailing in" to a geographically land-locked Bethlehem, "bearing our Savior Christ and His Laydee." In the "Cherry Tree Carol" Joseph bitterly—and so humanly—remonstrates with Mary, "Let the father of thy baby gather cherries for thee!" The "Holly and the Ivy," ancient Roman symbols of fertility, bear a "blood-red berry" and "prickly thorn" in tender imagery of Mary's birthing and poignant presentiment of Jesus' death.

In the Spanish carol "Fum, Fum, Fum!" one honors the birth of Christ by listing those cakes and candies available on the anniversary thereof. In "Hacia belén" a little donkey arrives in Bethlehem laden with chocolate, gypsies and a young man wearing a sombrero. "Maria, Maria, come quickly!" says the refrain, because "the chocolate is almost gone, the gypsies are stealing the swaddling clothes, and the donkey is eating the sombrero!"

A German love-song, extolling the faithful evergreen as a symbol of human love, has no trouble shifting its analogy to divine love in "O Tannenbaum."

With the exception of the Negro spiritual, America has developed few native Christmas carols, possibly because "the Pilgrim Fathers held the Puritan view as to the observance of the Church's seasons." But there is one affecting carol which John Jacob Niles relates he discovered on the Sunday afternoon of July 10, 1933 in Murphy, North Carolina, during the last meeting of a band of traveling evangelists. "Annie Morgan stood up," Niles recalled, "and, without benefit of any accompaniment, sang 'I wonder as I wander out under the sky,'" continuing (I would add) after the ancient and knowing tradition of the unknown folk-singers, "how Jesus the Savior did come for to die/for poor o'nery people like you and like I," not until the second verse touching at all the events of his birth.

Thus the carol grows, out of anonymous centuries of day-by-day longings and delights, clothed with a melodic grace approachable by only the most gifted of composers, and bearing imagery which but a few poets could achieve.

"If Jesus had wanted for any wee thing,
A star in the sky or a bird on the wing,
Or all of God's angels in heav'n for to sing,
He surely could have had it,
'cause His pappy was King."

Robert Shaw

I Saw Three Ships

Traditional English

Traditional English
Arr., John Stainer

5. O, they sailed in to Bethlehem,
On Christmas Day, on Christmas Day,
O, they sailed in to Bethlehem,
On Christmas Day in the morning.

6. And all the bells on earth shall ring,
On Christmas Day, on Christmas Day,
And all the bells on earth shall ring,
On Christmas Day in the morning.

7. And all the angels in heav'n shall sing,
On Christmas Day, on Christmas Day,
And all the angels in heav'n shall sing,
On Christmas Day in the morning.

8. And all the souls on earth shall sing,
On Christmas Day, on Christmas Day,
And all the souls on earth shall sing,
On Christmas Day in the morning.

9. Then let us all rejoice amain!
On Christmas Day, on Christmas Day,
Then let us all rejoice amain!
On Christmas Day in the morning.

Hallelujah! Unto Us

Richard Blank

Richard Blank

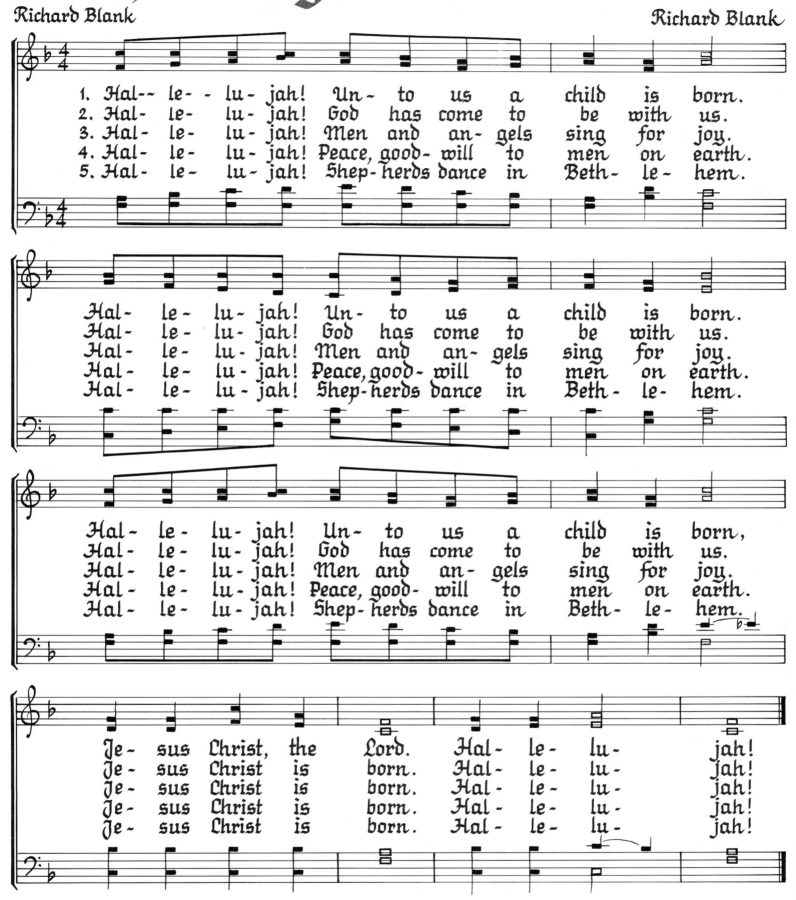

6. Hallelujah! Church bells ring out songs of praise.
Hallelujah! Church bells ring out songs of praise.
Hallelujah! Church bells ring out songs of praise.
Jesus Christ is born. Hallelujah!

7. Hallelujah! Hope arises in mankind.
Hallelujah! Hope arises in mankind.
Hallelujah! Hope arises in mankind.
Jesus Christ is born. Hallelujah!

8. Hallelujah! Unto us a child is born.
Hallelujah! Unto us a child is born.
Hallelujah! Unto us a child is born,
Jesus Christ, the Lord. Hallelujah!

Immanuel Is Born

Ron Klug

G. Winston Cassler

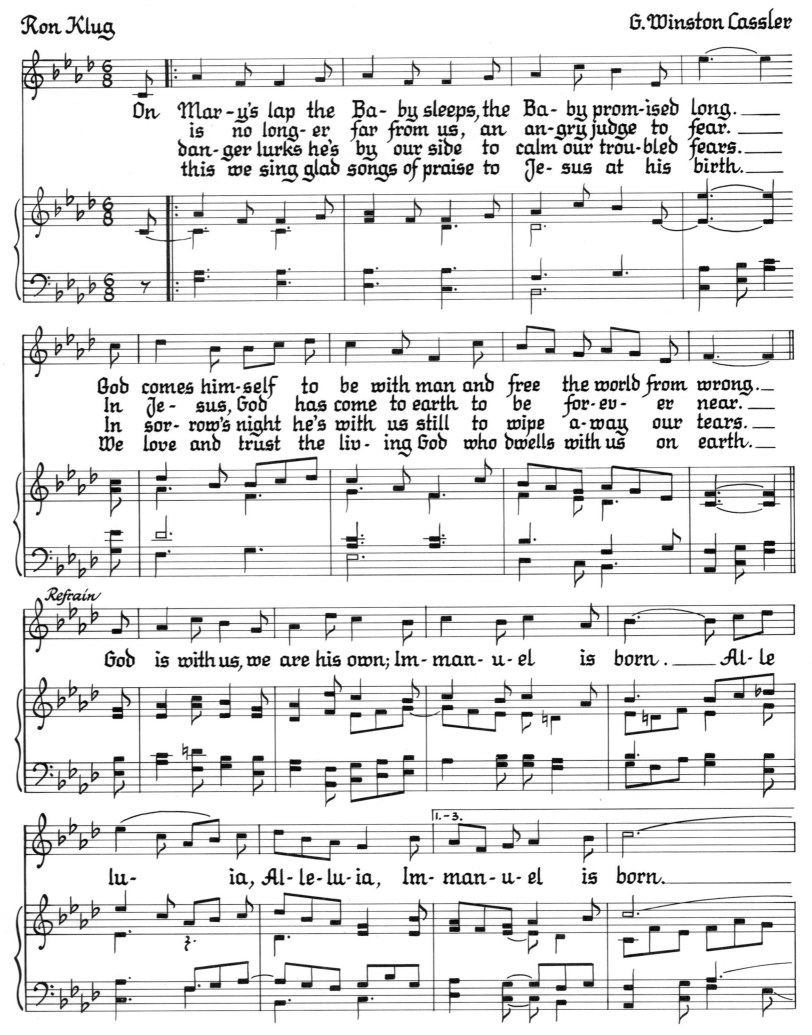

QUODLIBET ON
Silent Night and Away In a Manger

Franz Xaver Gruber, 1787-1863
19th Century American
Arr. Normand Lockwood

Matthew 21:9

Volemos, Pastorcitos
O Fly Now, Gentle Shepherds

Traditional Spanish
English translation, Mary Rose de Saettone

Traditional
Harm., David N. Johnson

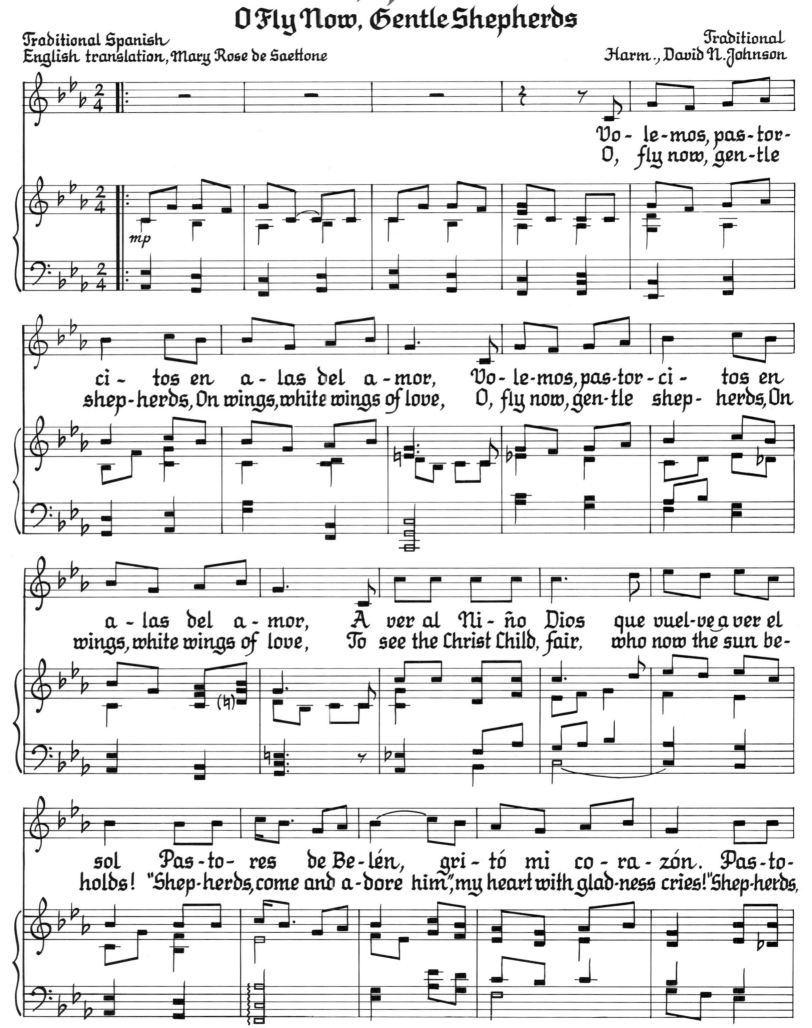

Vo - le-mos, pas-tor-ci - tos en a-las del a-mor, Vo - le-mos, pas-tor-ci - tos en
O, fly now, gen-tle shep-herds, On wings, white wings of love, O, fly now, gen-tle shep - herds, On

a - las del a - mor, A ver al Ni - ño Dios que vuel-ve a ver el
wings, white wings of love, To see the Christ Child, fair, who now the sun be-

sol Pas-to - res de Be - lén, gri - tó mi co - ra - zón. Pas-to-
holds! "Shep-herds, come and a-dore him", my heart with glad-ness cries!" Shep-herds,

res de Be- lén,___ gri- tó mi co- ra- zón.___
come and a- dore him", my heart with glad-ness cries!___

Child of Love

Richard Blank   Richard Blank

D   G   A   D

1. In   a sta- ble   long a- go a   ba- by boy was   born.
2. An- gel voic- es   in the wind pro- claimed the ho- ly   birth.
3. Sim- ple shep-herds in the field heard an- gel songs of joy.
4. There were wise-men in the east who read the heavns at night.
5. Winds and star told of a birth to those who sought God's will.

D   G   A   D   Refrain

Ev- 'ry year we cel- e- brate his birth on Christ-mas morn.
By   his pres-ence men would find the peace of God on   earth.
With the wind they jour-neyed forth to seek the new- born boy. Sing
By   the star of Beth- le- hem their lives were filled with light.
May the Child of Christ-mas morn with- in you al- ways dwell.

D   G   A   D   E   A

Al - le- lu- ia, Al- le- lu- ia. Blest is man by God a- bove. Sing

D   G   A   D   A   D

Al- le- lu- ia, Al- le- lu- ia. Glo- ry to the Child of love.

Lippai

Traditional Tyrolean Carol
Tr., George K. Evans

19th Century Tyrolean Carol
Harm., Robert Wetzler

Lip-pai, steh auf vom Schlaf! "Was ist denn da?" Mich
1. Lip-pai, get out of bed! "No, I'm a-sleep." There
2. He's born in Beth-le-hem. "How do you know?" The
3. No sweet-er, love-li-er Babe could I name. His

wun-dert's dass d' schla-fen kannst. "Ich schlaf' schon."
nev-er was such a sleep-y head! "Sleep-ing deep."
an-gels, I learned the place from them. "They told you so?"
bed noth-ing but a pile of hay, O, what a shame!

Geh mit mir auf die Weid', Schau, was für wun-der geit.
There is a glow in the night From a great star shin-ing bright!
Mar-y the blest moth-er mild, Ten-der-ly cares for her Child
Mar-y, if on-ly I might Hold the dear Sav-ior to-night,

'S ist so licht wie am Tag. "Was war das?"
See it is bright as day! "What did you say?"
There, 'neath the beam-ing star. "Can it be far?"
Pure joy I'd owe to you. "Please let me, too!"

Hand made two-story doll carousel made of tin, run by hand.

Nürnberg: German City of Toys

LA VERN J. RIPPLEY

Nürnberg is really Germany's Christmas City. Its annual *Christkindlesmarkt* is a kind of festival and bazaar where the Christian spirit of Christmas dovetails gently with commercialism. Every December 4th, in a square in front of the Church of Our Lady, booths open for business right after the nativity scene is re-enacted on the rear balcony of the famed edifice in a dazzling night-time pageant. Always the Biblical story comes first, the opening of the commercial stands follows. Later in the month a special torchlight parade further highlights the significance of the Christ child in Christmas, the true Light of the World. Other German cities also have Christmas markets, but nowhere is it so elegant, so famous, and so religiously oriented as in Nürnberg.

Nürnberg, however has the unofficial title of Germany's Christmas City for other reasons, namely the result of three local industries specially geared for Christmas: the making of ornaments, of baked goods, and of toys.

Once Germany produced virtually all the Christmas tree ornaments for world markets, a status symbol sacrificed permanently during World War II. The war-related interruption in supply prompted American glassmakers to perfect the high-speed machinery needed for mass production of such ornaments. In Germany ornament manufacturing grew up as a cottage industry scattered in the mountains and hills of Thuringia and Franconia. Whole families having ready access to the raw materials spent long days blowing and decorating them by hand. To be sure, some of this capacity for production passed away with the artisans and today much of the immediate ornament-producing area with its skilled populace lies behind the Iron Curtain.

Another industry that developed in Nürnberg, as a result of the availability of raw materials, was baking, particularly of sweet breads. During the Middle Ages the only known means to sweeten breads was honey, and Nürnberg was surrounded by pine forests in

61

which countless apiaries were operated from small cottages. In addition, Nürnberg's soils supported excellent grain products which were readily traded there due to the city's position on the major trade routes between Italy and the North Sea, Paris and Eastern Europe. Her location on the trade routes also assured Nürnberg bakers of excellent supplies of spices, vanilla, anise, cardamom, almonds, and dried fruit.

Today the whole world buys Nürnberg *Lebkuchen,* a large cookie that resembles a rich, moist biscuit. Often frosted now, Lebkuchen is still made of honey, flour, spices, and candied fruit. More deluxe versions call for ground almonds instead of the flour, however. Lebkuchen is a typical German Christmas gift, and producers have developed a toyland to spice up sales. Perhaps the most common one is a Lebkuchen witch's cottage from the story of "Hansel and Gretel." (Incidentally, according to the German version of this story, the house is not made of candy but of actual Lebkuchen.) There are also do-it-yourself kits of Lebkuchen, raw materials which can be constructed according to any child's whimsy. Often the Lebkuchen is shipped in cans painted with colorful scenes of old Nürnberg or in "treasure chests" filled with assorted cakes and cookies made from Lebkuchen.

Perhaps the most fundamental Christmas industry of Nürnberg is one that gladdens the hearts of children everywhere, namely, toys. The first Nürnberg toy to gain fame in Europe was the ordinary doll. To children, dolls are, of course, "people." Thus ancillary industries quickly developed to "house" the doll "families." Soon doll houses became enormously popular, prompting German artisans in Nürnberg to build the most intricate reproductions of reality: real windows, real wall paper, real scale-modeled dresses, suits of silk and lace, all complemented with beads and ornaments. Mostly the figures were carved from wood, but in the neighboring city of Fürth, slightly west of Nürnberg, workmen pioneered in the production of tin figures. Fürth eventually became famous in its own right for its tin soldiers. Its barnyard and woodlot animals also garnered for the city an excellent reputation.

As for Nürnberg itself, its most simple and yet most successful invention was the spinning top. Forgotten now but once equally famous was the Nürnberg peep show. It was made like a box or an egg which the child could hold up to the light and look inside through a magnifying lens which revealed, for example, a magnificent Venetian canal or a splendid mountain range. As long ago as 1600, Nürnbergers were also crafting mechanical toys. But extensive application of these early arts was not possible until the industrial revolution permitted production on a grand scale.

Among other ingenious toys to come from the craftsmen of Nürnberg were some that were later labeled as "scandalous." There was one, for example, in which the figures nodded their heads, wagged their jaws, and ambled about. With no clock mechanism, people were mystified about the power source. Eventually the humane were surprised to find that a tightly caged bird served as the "motor." Not unlike some of our war-oriented toymakers today, a Nürnberger living during the French Revolution turned out what Goethe's mother described as a "murder machine," actually a model guillotine complete with a doll for decapitation.

Thank goodness there has been some improvement in what objectives toy manufacturers have for their wares today. According to Professor Hans Mieskes, who is the author of *Gutes Spielzeug* (The Good Toy), a handbook published by the German Federal Republic, toy makers have 13 different categories of "educational playthings." Essentially, they say, a toy should help a child broaden and intensify his experiences of the environment. Whether instructional or just plain fun, a toy should permit the free play of a child's imagination. Thus, according to Mieskes, the size of toys should, generally speaking, be in inverse proportion to the child. Small children need bigger objects such as cars, blocks, and balls, while older children with greater dexterity need smaller items to refine their skills. If possible, toys should be logically constructed so that children can figure out just how they function. The material out of which the toy is made, however, is immaterial. Wood, plastic, fabric,

The Toy Museum in Nürnberg dates back to the second half of the nineteenth century.

The first floor of the museum displays toys of wood and plastic.

metal, all can be used for good or bad toys. With today's ecologists admonishing our throw-away society, the Germans counsel adults to begin ecological training with the child by purchasing sturdy toys that do not break the first time they're used. "Play value" and "life expectancy" should therefore be the prime factors in toy selection.

While "play" is the most important objective for toys, Nürnberg's children have been fascinated with a new toy museum which opened its doors in 1971. The museum is mostly for looking and offers little actual playing. The children do not mind, however, for their parents enjoy "just looking" as well. Housed in an impressive patrician house, the museum overlooks the central market near the historical *Schöner Brunnen* (Beautiful Fountain) behind the Church of Our Lady. Displaying both current items as well as older displays from the history of toymaking, the museum is particularly proud of its 2,000-year-old bronze dice from Athens and its 500-year-old clay dolls. Glazed clay figures of knights on horseback were commonplace toys in medieval Germany. Supposedly, war-toys were a natural preparation for the arts of chivalry, and in the royal families young boys often received wooden cannons and gold man-on-horse figures.

Another medieval toy that has enjoyed perennial popularity is the hobby-horse. Seemingly, the hobby-horse gained permanent stature in the toy world as a result of children seeing their fathers forever on horseback. With hobby horses children staged their own tournaments and jousting meets, at least, so we must conclude from the marginal pictures painted in certain manuscripts of the *Book of Hours*.

Some historians believe that the development of toymaking in Nürnberg and southern Germany was closely associated with religious art. We know, for example, that in the south German villages of Berchtesgaden and Oberammergau, wood carvers dedicated to making religious figures for their créches turned to producing other figures which were sold as toys. Some authorities even claim that the créche was once strictly a Catholic child's toy. Having plenty of wood and talent in their alpine environment, these Bavarians perfected the arts of both carving and painting the wood. For a time in the 16th century, in fact, these winter whittlers proved a real commercial threat to the toy guild workers in Nürnberg. The market place remained in Nürnberg, however. And when small towns surrounding Nürnberg tried to copy the arts of the religious carvers from Oberammergau and Berch-

Glass Case: Toys from Peru, Columbia and North America
Background: Toys from Africa, Java and Japan

Doll carriage, about 1914; Toy children's car, 1905;
Hand carved rocking horse, 1923 and various marionettes
from old Nürnberg marionette theater

Well furnished Doll Kitchen, Augsburg about 1800,
dining room was added later, about 1850

tesgaden, hoping to be more competitive by being closer to the main markets, they failed because they had not yet perfected watercolors for use on wood.

Thus for decades while the toy suppliers were in the deep south of Germany, salesmen fanned out from Nürnberg to peddle their wares to retailers in the principal cities of Europe. German toys were in great demand in Venice as early as 1566. And judging from royal family accounts, toys for children of the celebrated were often ordered directly from the German carvers or craftsmen. For example, silver toy soldiers were made in the city of Nürnberg in 1672 for Louis XIV's children. Even in William Penn's colony in America, German craftsmen were recognized for making wooden toys and painting them in styles still known to this day under the heading of "folk art."

German toys were often religious in nature. For instance, we know of doll-house models of the marriage feast of Cana and elaborate sets of Noah's Ark with the many pairs of animals. More popular items, however, included the rocking horse, and after 1775, especially, the *Zinnsoldaten*, or the tin soldiers, a name that persists in popular speech even today when better metals and alloys are substituted for "tin" soldiers. The military achievements of Frederick the Great seem to have given a major impetus to "toy soldiering," so much so that in the Nürnberg of that day Johann Gottfried Hilpert alone made 40 types of Frederick's soldiers. By 1800 there were at least 80 toy foundries in Fürth, all occupied predominately with making military toys. Once found in every home, the Nürnberg toy soldier has become today at least as important for the adult collector as it was once for the child.

If military toys were somehow typically German, they appealed nevertheless to children around the globe. Even more indigenous to the German cultural tilt than military 'hardware' was the miniature toy theater. And although fascination for miniature theaters was widespread, it was the Nürnberger and the Augsburger graphic and printing artists who perfected a parallel business, namely, of the Magic Lantern. Varying in type from a version of our kaleidoscope to stereoscopic panoramas and dioramas, the shows amounted to little more than painted cloth transparencies whose scenes were projected for the audience by a light shining from the rear of the frame. All of this is, of course, rooted in the German love for theater and in the fondness of German children for puppetry. Goethe, as is well known, had a childhood passion for the toy theater as well as for puppetry and recounted his personal experiences as the character *Wilhelm Meister* speaking to Marianne.

In 19th century Germany, in fact, the marionette theater was taken so seriously that professional authors wrote for it, thus enhancing the wealth of a repertoire that had previously been handed down orally. In Ulm and Cologne, for instance, the marionette theaters made great use of local situations and dialects with high success, while at Hamburg it was the hand puppet theater that flourished throughout the middle of the century. Often actors and players achieved distinction not for their acting in person but for their puppet performances. Where local talent failed, to be sure, there were plenty of stock pieces for the local puppet theaters. Often puppet theater talent was enjoyed for more than its toy quality as parents and grown-ups increasingly grew willing to pay to see the puppet performers.

Be that as it may, the melodramatic streak in their titles suggests that the fanciful was always uppermost in the mind of the author, as illustrated by these: *The King of the Alps and the Enemy of Man; The Death Bell at Midnight; The Murder in the Wine Cellar; The Devil's Mill on the Viennese Hills.* Biblical themes such as *Goliath and David, Judith,* and *Christmas Hills* were always popular as was the figure of Kasper. Kasper is a cunning, affectionate, comic, and commonsense character alive to social protest and popular acclamation. The Kasper and the Hampelmann (Jumping Jack) were ubiquitous characters in all of German puppetry.

While Nürnberg toymakers seem to have garnered a reputation for their dolls, they also supplied the highly popular "Nürnberg Kitchen" which was sold under that label all over the world. Likewise, toy trains puffed around the nursery bend in the latter half of the 19th century and have been tooting and chugging in living rooms ever since. Old catalogues of certain Nürnberg firms also show wide varieties of wooden building toys. When mechanization took over from the older artisans, the wide use of folk-art in toy making began to recede while optical and mechanical toys rose in prominence. Catalogues from such famous firms as Bestelmeier contain entries ranging up to 1200 in varieties of toys available.

Two individuals who nudged the toymaking industry into new roadways were Ernest Froebel, an architect who opened the first kindergarten in Germany in 1837, and Dr. Maria Montessori, noted for her pre-kindergarten Montessori schools. Froebel proceeded from the principle that "if you can help it, never deprive the child of the sacred right of discovery" or in short, "learn by doing." Montessori, on the other hand, rests her theories on a child's spontaneous interest in work, noting that children love order and repetition and that they look on their play as a kind of work. Construction toys, number games, and wide varieties of instructional toys trace their origins in one way or another to these two innovators.

As might be expected, the Christmas season itself inspired many German toys. Nürnberg and Alpine carvers delighted in making angels and carolers not only for Nativity scenes but also for children to play with. The Seiffen workshops created large figures of the "child angel," its long white dress sparsely ornamented with dots from a paint brush. Its crown, interestingly, was shaped and colored like a miner's headgear. On some models, extra candles on the platform turned a turbine wheel making a little bell tinkle in

Different costume dolls. In the lower part an Algerian Refugee Child by Sasha Morgenthaler, about 1950. Upper, a doll's wash house from about 1920, and a walking doll clothed in white

A pull horse with drums, from Grodner Valley. Doll carriage pre-1914; Doll, 1885; Biedermeier doll around 1840; Sled, from eighteenth century

Hand-made team for canon in the style of a Bavarian field model from the last quarter of the nineteenth century. The wooden headed soldiers helmets and sabers, etc., are all hand made

rhythm while three small miners twist and turn. No other combination of sound, sight, movement, and religious sentiment could make a better Christmas toy.

The miner's influence on this art reflects the proximity to Nürnberg of the Erzgebirge, a mountain range where mining was once a mainstay of life. Wholesale adaptation of the Christmas créche to the local scene, in fact, was fashionable in many areas of Germany. Thus the Lord's birth was presented in a miner's cottage, a farm house, a charcoal-burner's hut, and many other domestic scenes to stress the common humanity of the traditional Christmas story. From these humble beginnings, it appears, the more professional toymakers of Nürnberg pioneered a whole array of toys.

German toymakers also invented the continuous movement toy, or the "endless band toy." A common one was "the girl chasing geese" which was produced by the Seiffen makers. Similarly, the Germans were among the first with miniature sewing machines, typewriters, and of course working steam engines. The next stage brought the toy automobile, although the toy gasoline engine was not so easily reproduced. Instead the wind-up clockwork toy grew to maturity, furnishing power for distinguished contemporary German cars. Besides cars, German toy catalogues from the turn of the century also show some elaborate train depot setups, of which a few clockwork models were available as early as the 1860s. Workable toy telephones also made the scene early, probably in the 1870s. Led by the Bing Makers of Nürnberg, the exact art of scale modeling was honed with such finesse that these products have been called miniature "poems in metal." The very first model electric railway (actually a streetcar) was developed by Carette of Nürnberg in 1893. The early models first used batteries, then siphoned power from an unreliable lamp resistance mechanism run off the house supply.

The tinkertoy was an American invention, but German toy factories were in the forefront with construction toys of similar types. These included metal elements, wood blocks, and paper parts. Vehicles, airplanes, ships, animals, and houses were also available in varying styles.

Various technological toys, locomotives, steam machines with horizontal or vertical engines, and power sources from different manufacturers in the first quarter of the 20th century

To get the best "picture" of what toys the City of Nürnberg had and still has to offer the world, one must pay a personal visit to *Das Spielzeugmuseum der Stadt Nürnberg,* number 13 Karl Street. A structure that once housed the Nürnberg toy business of Schrögler & Scheckenbach, the property was acquired by the city in 1961 with the provision that it be made into a museum for toys. Not until 1967 did planning take serious shape, however. To best serve the interested public, the displays in the museum are arranged around such themes as "Buildings and Building Units," "Travel and Vehicles of Travel," "Doll houses, Doll rooms, and Doll kitchens," "Doll dishes," "Children's Theater, Marionettes, and Optical Toys," and "Tin and Mechanical Toys," the latter being further divided into groups of electrical, steam, or spring powered toys. From the very beginning, the museum was intended as a museum dedicated to the "world" of toys and thus it does not focus on Nürnberg only, nor for that matter, exclusively on Germany. Toys on display come from everywhere, including Peru, Africa, Java, India, and Japan.

A few more eye-catching items in the museum include a 1915 windup model of a tin ambulance, and some Lilliputian paratroopers. Beautiful mechanically as well as artistically are the model trains. Corresponding to these pieces are the pre-motorized vehicles, for instance, the Imperial German mail coaches complete with horse teams and scale-model horse barns. The doll houses illustrate not only delicate dinner service for the guests, but excellent waffle irons, pudding forms, and even a doll's cookbook. In the Children's Theater we have complete stages, curtains, props for the stage and doll actors putting on this or that fairytale for an audience. The doll display itself exhibits virtually unlimited variety in both doll figures and styles of clothing. The section dedicated to the "wooden toys" is representative of the German areas distinguished for their wood carving talents. Not to be overlooked is the department on games and magical devices.

Perhaps the single individual who has done most to make the Toy Museum a reality and a success has been Dr. Lydia Bayer, the present curator. She and her mother, Mrs. Lydia Bayer Sr. of Würzburg, spent decades assembling toys into a private museum in their own home. No doubt the best overall source of information about the history of toymaking in Nürnberg is a dissertation on the topic by Dr. Georg Wenzel. (This item was available to me only as an abbreviated article entitled "Die Geschichte der Nürnberger Spielzeugindustrie," as serialized in the magazine *Das Spielzeug* beginning with the June, 1968 number).

Having lived up to its reputation so admirably over the centuries, the city of Nürnberg today annually hosts the largest toy fair in the world. February 1971 witnessed the 22nd consecutive annual trade fair at which 1,357 firms from all over the world assembled to display their toys and take orders for delivery the

A doll with a china head and Baiersdorf costume rides a pull horse; in the background is the museum

following Christmas. While 847 of the firms came from West and East Germany, the United States was represented by 24, Italy by 99, Great Britain by 94, France by 61, and Japan by 24, with one from the Soviet Union. Some 20,000 buyers came, evaluated the wares, and bought what they saw, thus contributing to the 1.4 billion DM per year toy industry in Germany.

Not only is Nürnberg the mercantile center of the industry, it is also the brain center for the toymaker's associations, toy dealer's associations, and the toy maker's labor unions. The city, renowned for its churches, is also famous for its artists, among them Albrecht Dürer, Adam Kraft, and Veit Stoss. The most famous masterpiece of the latter, hanging in the Lorenz Church, is a beautiful wood carving of the Annunciation to Mary that she would bear Jesus, as if rounding out the prerequisites for Nürnberg to gain the reputation of Germany's Christmas city.

Volume I - 1931

Volume II - 1932

Volume III - 1933

Volume IV - 1934

Volume V - 1935

Volume VI - 1936

Volume VII - 1937

Volume VIII - 1938

Volume IX - 1939

Volume X - 1940

CHRISTMAS

1973

Volume XI - 1941

Volume XII - 1942

Volume XIII - 1943

Volume XIV - 1944

Volume XV - 1945

CHRISTMAS 1973 represents forty-three years of continuous publication in the field of Christmas literature and art. Randolph E. Haugan, founder and editor of the volume, has through the years ferreted out new themes related to Christmas which have been developed by writers, composers, and artists, and has made other selections from materials which have come unsolicited. The type is set in Linotype Caledonia. Headings are set in Monotype Goudy Blackletter with Lombardic initials. This volume is printed by photo-offset Lithography and published by Augsburg Publishing House, Minneapolis, Minnesota.

- -

Volume XVI - 1946

Volume XVII - 1947

Volume XVIII - 1948

Volume XIX - 1949

Volume XX - 1950

Volume XXI - 1951

Volume XXII - 1952

Volume XXIII - 1953

Volume XXIV - 1954

Volume XXV - 1955

Volume XXVI -1956

Volume XXVII - 1957

Volume XXVIII - 1958

Volume XXIX - 1959

Volume XXX - 1960

Volume XXXI - 1961

Volume XXXII - 1962

Volume XXXIII - 1963

Volume XXXIV - 1964

Volume XXXV - 1965

Volume XXXVI - 1966

Volume XXXVII - 1967

Volume XXXVIII - 1968

Volume XXXIX - 1969

Volume XL - 1970

Volume XLI - 1971

Volume XLII - 1972